# THE SOUL OF KAZAKHSTAN

# THE SOUL OF

## KAZAKHSTAN

## PHOTOGRAPHS BY

## ESSAYS BY ALMA KUNANBAY
## EDITED BY GARETH L. STEEN

## DESIGN BY BILL McCAFFERY

PUBLISHED BY
EASTEN PRESS
NEW YORK, NEW YORK AND SARASOTA, FLORIDA

Translated into English by Aylin Abayhan
and Uli Schamiloglu

Edited by Gareth L. Steen

Consulting editors: Muzafar Alimbaev,
Talasbek Asemkulov, Izaly Zemtsovsky, Ron Weber
Kazakh edition edited by Talasbek Asemkulov
Russian edition edited by Izaly Zemtsovsky

Research and captions by Patricia Eastep

Produced by Gareth L. Steen
Words at Play Editorial and Creative Services
Cape Canaveral, Florida

Design Director, Bill McCaffery
New York, New York

Library of Congress Cataloging-in-Publication Data
Eastep, Wayne.
The Soul of Kazakhstan/photographs by Wayne Eastep; text by Alma Kunanbay;
edited by Gareth L. Steen; design by Bill McCaffery.
p. cm.
ISBN 0-9706939-0-7
1. Kazakhstan—Social life and customs—Pictorial works.
2. Kazakhstan—Civilization—Pictorial works. I. Kunanbay, Alma, 1949- II. Steen, Gareth L.
III. McCaffery, William. IV. Title.

DK906 .E17 2001
958.45—dc21
00-067677

Printed in China

Published by
EASTEN PRESS
New York, New York and Sarasota, Florida

Notes: 1) Many Kazakh geographic regions, landmarks, cities and towns, streets and avenues, individual's names, etc. are now known by their Kazakh names and spellings rather than their Soviet-era designations. The Kazakh names have been used in this book in most cases. Since there is not yet a standardized English transliteration for some of these names, the most commonly used Kazakh spellings have been used in this volume. 2) Most metric conversions have been rounded off.

To the readers of *The Soul of Kazakhstan:*

Vast steppes alternating with forests and deserts, mountains and seas, lakes and rivers, form the territory of modern Kazakhstan. Ours is an extremely beautiful country, rich in history and culture and unique in natural landscapes. These bear evidence of ancient civilizations that are still reflected in our modern times.

This is the area traversed in the past by the Great Silk Road, along which were prosperous cities with highly developed social structures, crafts and trade, as well as a rural sector engaged in livestock-breeding and farming. But now our major wealth is in our people. Many generations of Kazakhstanis, who protected and created the treasures of our country, as well as shepherding its potential, live and work here today. It is they who represent the real soul of Kazakhstan, which now celebrates the 10th anniversary of its independence.

This book has many merits: Key is its illumination of our people as they aspire to make our country even more beautiful and prosperous, as well as its expertly made photographs that fully and brilliantly capture the intrinsic color of this land and encourage love and respect towards it. This volume offers a fresh look at our past and present, and at the invaluable heritage and wealth that must be further cultivated and passed along to the next generations.

Kazakhstan's future at the intersection of the European West and the Asian East is bright. Amidst this Eurasian space, it plays an ever-increasing role in the political, economic, commercial, transport and communications bridge between the countries of this region. We are open to efficient cooperation with other states of the world. We have established business partnerships and relations with many major multinational corporations working for the common benefit. Among them is Exxon Mobil Corporation, the initiator of this publication.

I believe this book will expand the circle of our friends and partners. It will also assist anyone who sincerely desires to discover for himself or herself the soul of our diverse and unique world, which has entered the 21st century as the Republic of Kazakhstan. With best wishes,

Nursultan Nazarbaev
President of the Republic of Kazakhstan

Kazakhstan has many dimensions. It stretches from the Caspian Sea to China and from the Tien Shan mountains to Siberia. It is the world's ninth largest country, sprawled across the heart of the vast Eurasian steppes, the grassy lands that once served as the highway of the legendary Silk Road and the home of nomadic equestrian peoples.

It is a nation with a history spanning the millennia and a cultural heritage among the world's richest and most diverse. With independence in 1991 the country began a rebirth – a reemergence and a rediscovery of its heritage and its soul.

Under its first Kazakh leader this century, President Nursultan Nazarbaev, the country is coming into its own and has once again become an economic center of Central Asia. It is rich in natural and mineral resources. ExxonMobil subsidiaries have been active in Kazakhstan since 1993. We helped evaluate the country's hydrocarbon potential and we are continuing to invest in petroleum exploration and production opportunities. We also market fuels and lubricants. ExxonMobil has developed a productive and important business partnership with Kazakhstan, a relationship we will remain committed to for many years to come.

But moreover, ExxonMobil tries to be a good corporate citizen and an integral part of the countries and communities where our employees live and work. This book, four years in the making, is one of a number of cultural and community projects we have undertaken in Kazakhstan over the years. On this tenth anniversary of independence, this book is intended to tell about Kazakhstan's rich, reemerging heritage and to provide windows into the many facets that make up the soul of Kazakhstan, its humanity and its heritage.

We would like to thank the talented team that produced this volume and all those who assisted and advised inside and outside of ExxonMobil divisions and affiliates. It is our hope that readers everywhere will enjoy, savor and learn from these wonderful and insightful photographs, captions and essays.

Lee R. Raymond
CEO and Chairman, ExxonMobil

Winter snows blanket the Kazakh steppes, and the line between earth and sky fades as a soft quiet fills the air. Many see the vastness of this open space as emptiness. Kazakhs see freedom, beauty, peace and serenity.

Spring spreads a veil of white apple blossoms across the foothills that lead from the steppes up to the mountain ranges of the Tien Shan and Altai. Tulips, blood-red, and sun-yellow, punctuate the landscape as if to announce that something special is coming.

Summer arrives with an explosion of red poppies, carnations and roses. From start to finish a carpet of wild flowers covers the summer landscape. The wind, wave upon wave, moves through the silvery feather grass and pale-green sage on the steppes.

Autumn pulls a coat of many colors onto the backs of the foothills – the golds, reds and oranges of the wild apricot, barberry and birch. They are framed by the white of the high mountain peaks and the soft gray-green sage of the steppes.

Kazakhstan is a land blessed with natural riches, which have sustained the Kazakhs in their struggles and lifted their spirits. Kazakh poets, playwrights, writers and musicians have reflected through epic song and ballad this strong relationship with nature. The expression of faith through Tengrism, shamanism, Sufism, and Zoroastrianism has created rituals and ideas that reflect a deep relationship with nature.

A wise elder said to me once, "God gave Kazakhstan its many natural riches so we would have strength to handle the many difficulties to come our way." The difficulties included invasion by the Mongols under Chingis Khan and the destruction of the great library at Otrar. During the Soviet era they included damage to the Aral Sea, the testing of over 400 atomic bombs near Semey, submission of traditional Kazakh culture under the heel of Stalinism and the "Red Eagle" purge of the 1930s.

Across the centuries traders have followed the ancient routes of the Silk Road crisscrossing the vast steppes. Today managers of multinationals continue that business tradition and have helped make Kazakhstan once again the commercial center of Central Asia.

Kazakhstan has been home and nurturer to seminal thinkers and has played a significant role in history. It is the place where people first rode the horse and today cosmonauts ride Soyuz rockets from Baikonyr into space. The apple was first cultivated in Kazakhstan and the tulip we associate with Holland has its home here. For millennia Kazakh women have been warriors and chiefs.

The characteristic that stood out to me as one of the strengths of Kazakhstan is the generous spirit of the Kazakh people. My family and I were always made to feel welcome. People opened their homes, hearts and minds, and shared with us their ideas, feelings and delicious food. After each of our encounters we felt our bodies nourished, our minds expanded, our spirits uplifted and our hearts warmed.

Upon my arrival in Kazakhstan I sensed I was in a special place. The first morning I was taken on an introductory drive around Almaty. As we climbed a mountain slope at the edge of the city we came upon small trees covered with pieces of cloth tied to the branches, which was generally accepted to be an expression of good luck by couples getting married. As we continued our drive, we came upon other trees – in the mountains and near streams – that were also tied with cloth.

The next week I met Dr. Khalel Argynbayev, president of the Academy of Science and director of its Department of History, who was to brief me on Kazakh history and culture. Toward the end of our visit I mentioned the trees I'd seen and asked if they had any meaning beyond good luck wishes. Without hesitation he answered, "Yes, they have important meaning and represent the core of traditional Kazakh culture and its worldview. These sites are always near water – particularly moving water, rivers or streams – and are often in the mountains. The tree represents the tree of life and is a connection between Mother Earth and the sky, the realm of our ancestors and the Great Spirit. The pieces of cloth are prayer cloths. This practice of tying the prayer cloths on the trees is an expression of our fundamental connection to nature."

I told him the trees had caught my attention because I'd recently been to a sun dance ceremony with the Sioux on the Pine Ridge Reservation in South Dakota. They also tie prayer cloths onto a tree, which is placed in the center of the sun dance circle, and it is a symbol with similar meaning. He advised me to pay careful attention in my travels to rituals the people practice, like these, because they are examples of the deep roots of Kazakh culture.

When I arrived in Kazakhstan in the fall of 1997, the Jubilee Celebration for one of Kazakhstan's great writers, Mukhtar Äuezov, was being held. The celebrations began in Semey in the north. I boarded a bus that was to take us from Semey out to Borli, the place of Äuezov's home village, and quickly discovered I had inadvertently gotten onto the VIP bus. I sat down next to a soft-spoken man, Dr. Murat Äuezov, the son of the writer being honored. Our conversation moved quickly into a spirited and impassioned discussion about the influences that helped define Kazakh culture, worldview and faith:

Tengrism, which sees a unity between the earth, human experience and the realm of the spirit; veneration of ancestors; shamanism, a belief in good and evil spirits that can be influenced by shamans; Zoroastrianism, which sees a universal struggle between the forces of light and darkness; and Sufism, a mystical practice that uses poetry, music and dance to express one's faith. He urged me to visit a number of places where I would see examples of these influences: the region around Qïzïlorda, the mountain Khan-Tengri, and the underground temple of Shakbak-Ata.

Following the advice I'd been given, I traveled to these and many other special places. In each place my contacts with Kazakhs were remarkable encounters marked by passionate engagement and the sharing of feelings and ideas about the important concerns of life. Time after time people moved beyond the abstract exploration of ideas to a way of life infused with the practical application of their "faith."

The title for this book was chosen very carefully. A soul is the union of the body and the spirit. We wanted to illuminate ways in which the spirit of the people and nature of the land have interacted to create the soul of Kazakhstan. Each person whose image appears in this book, and those left out only because of space limitations, represents a significant contribution. They have opened themselves up to my camera and allowed me to capture their spirit.

None of this could have been accomplished without the help of scores of individuals. The names of many of them appear on the Acknowledgments page, but others deserve special mention. The support of Dana Suyundikova and Irina Serkebaeva, who acted as on-the-ground coordinators and interpreters, Alexander (Sasha) Amelin, guide and driver, and many others on the staff of ExxonMobil Kazakhstan, Inc. (EMKI), was immeasurable. Likewise, the support, freedom and trust EMKI gave me deserve enthusiastic recognition. And I will be forever grateful to David Goodner for his vision, support and guidance.

During the course of this project it was my privilege to witness firsthand the renaissance of the rich Kazakh culture that is currently taking place. My hope is that the images in *The Soul of Kazakhstan* will open windows into a beautiful and inspiring land and illuminate a remarkable people who opened their hearts and minds to share a love of their heritage.

Wayne Eastep

How does one set out to accomplish the somewhat presumptuous task of trying to capture and illuminate the soul of a country and people? First, with a great deal of deliberation and caution, and second, with a sensitive and insightful team of experts who feel both daunted and inspired by the job before them.

Producing and editing cultural books is always a privilege and a journey. As the voyage of *The Soul of Kazakhstan* proceeded, its route proved to be longer and more adventurous than most. Any such project poses challenges and difficulties, and this one had its share of peaks and valleys. But each setback had its breakthrough and every question a corresponding epiphany.

What kept us going when we ran into obstacles were experiences and people – or the memory of them – who added to our joy and understanding. A picnic, for example, turned into a sharing of philosophies on an autumn afternoon in a hilly apple orchard outside Almaty with the Tien Shan Mountains providing a monumental backdrop. While visiting fjord-like Kul-Say with rank on rank of 100-foot-tall firs mounting the lake's steep palisades like dark green exclamation points, we unexpectedly came upon an old Tengri ceremonial site atop a nearby mountaintop. There was a star-filled night crossing of the steppes with a lone wolf – a Kazakh totem for centuries – on sentry along a rutted, two-track road. There were conversations with new friends who guided us in the rediscovery of lost or enshrouded history and who helped unravel cultural and religious mysteries. At sometimes quiet and sometimes effervescent dinners in Kazakh homes and yurts, we listened to music and shared ideas and enjoyed legendary Kazakh hospitality. Outside Kazakhstan, there were intense and intensive meetings in Berkeley, California; Madison, Wisconsin; Sarasota, Florida; and New York City.

And, in the end, each turn in the road seemed designed for one purpose: to bring the present team together.

Wayne Eastep brings sensitivity and a fine eye to his photographic art. Although we hadn't worked together before, an affinity and friendship had developed over several years; and when this opportunity arose, he seemed just the right man for the job. Just how suited he was didn't become fully apparent until he hit the ground in Kazakhstan. Eastep's photographs tell of a man who fell in love with a country and its people. He – and at various times his wife and partner, Patti, and his assistant, Bill DeVincenzo – spent a total of nearly a year covering Kazakhstan's vast reaches in four trips. In their travels they talked with and photographed people who are experts in their fields as well as ordinary folk along the way – farmers and herders, eagle men and horsemen, nomads and urban dwellers, professors and historians, shamans and doctors, artists and craftsmen, composers and epic singers, and dancers and instrumentalists. In so doing, Wayne got beneath the surface and developed a rapport with the people. He also discovered in their heritage threads of history and culture with intriguing links to his own American Indian ancestry.

Wayne and his team often photographed for 20 hours at a time. They slept in snatches, traveled in helicopters and jeeps, climbed mountains, forded streams, visited villagers and government officials, and partook in many vodka toasts. Wayne's tireless work and dedication soon uncovered the pictorial substance of the soul we were after.

After a lengthy search, Dr. Alma Kunanbay was recommended by several Kazakh and American academicians. This turned out to be either serendipity or fate, since Dr. Kunanbay seemingly spent much of her professional life as an anthropologist, ethnographer and historian getting ready to open a window to make accessible her country's culture and ethos – indeed, its very soul. As an ethnic Kazakh who married a Russian academician, she says she found her voice and her roots in the writing of the text that accompanies each chapter of this book. In fact, upon completion of the manuscript, she changed the spelling of her name from the Russianized Kunanbayeva, to the Kazakh Kunanbay. Alma – which means "apple" in Kazakh – is the embodiment of an Earth Mother: brilliant, warm, caring and soothing. She marshaled her facts, her thoughts and her feelings about her heritage and gave them a stirring and meaningful depth.

Designer Bill McCaffery, a 1996 inductee into the Art Directors' Hall of Fame, also found an affinity with Wayne's images and Alma's text. His fresh and bold design captures the underlying ethos of the project.

Aylin Abayhan and Uli Schamiloglu who translated Dr. Kunanbay's text into English, Izaly Zemtsovsky who edited the Russian edition, Talasbek Asemkulov who edited the Kazakh edition, and Muzafar Alimbaev and Ron Weber who were consulting editors, all brought their talent and their hearts to this project. And the man at its genesis was David Goodner; without his heartfelt support and astute guidance, this book would not have come to fruition.

The result of all these labors is a book that melds a text rich in history and insight with photographs that mirror that traditional heritage as reflected in the faces of 21$^{st}$ century Kazakhstan. This does not mean a book full of photographs of Almaty's wide boulevards and stately government and academic buildings, or its modern hotels and discos, boutiques and galleries and cafes and restaurants at the turn of this century; nor does it show the burgeoning of Astana, the new capital of Kazakhstan, where ministries and parks and soccer fields and sports stadiums are taking shape, and a gleaming new capitol building will soon rise.

What it does depict, in both photographs and text, are the glowing, expectant faces of youth, and the history and tradition those young Kazakh eyes and minds are rediscovering. It portrays contemporary religion and art and performance, but in the context of how Kazakh life and culture from centuries and millennia past have shaped the face and soul of Kazakhstan today, a heritage that is once again providing both a subtext and a structure for a society attuned to its own voice.

This book is a fond and insightful look into the Kazakh culture – a primer, if you will, of many of the aspects that comprise a particularly warm and wonderful people who make the soul of this country so unique.

Gareth L. Steen

The book that you are opening is not just an album of photographs with captioned text. Nor is it simply a voyage to far-away, exotic places. It is something more – the result of the opening of a civilization that is still unknown to much of the world: the civilization of the Kazakhs, one of the nomadic peoples of Eurasia.

Kazakhstan, situated in the geographic center of Eurasia, has been well known since the times of the Great Silk Road. It combines today, just as it did during that distant epoch, features that are remarkable for their contrasts: East and West, modernism and archaism, impetuous youth and the staid wisdom of ancestors. The limitless expanses of the country encompass countless natural riches. The perpetually snow-capped mountains thrusting up to the heavens are neighbors of the Great Steppe; the regions of the picturesque lakes – the so-called eyes of the earth – and the rivers filled with water are surrounded by neighboring desert. The variety and contrast of Kazakhstan's landscapes give rise to the possibility of sensing such basic fundamental cultural ideas as Eternity and Beauty. However, only a deep familiarity with Kazakh nomadic civilization allows one to not only sense, but to understand, how these fundamental ideas are philosophically thought out, formulated and artistically realized in traditional Kazakh culture. As a result, becoming familiar with the nomadic world of the Kazakhs encompasses unexpected discoveries and inspiring revelations that at the same time prove to be one of the most reliable paths even to self-understanding.

Work on this book became such a discovery and revelation for me. A quarter-century ago, having completed my training and equipped with the knowledge received in a European system of education under the tutelage of the late teacher Asiya Esimovna Baygaskina, I first encountered face to face the sources of my own culture. I soon learned that I had a lot to learn! It was truly the beginning of a long, difficult, and happy voyage to the wellsprings of my own nomadic civilization. Such a voyage at the same time proved to be a return to and a restoration of one's self – the rebirth of memory, so to speak. I am happy that in my lifetime this coincided with the rebirth of my country, which regained independence a decade ago.

Independence begins with the reawakening of ethnic self-awareness within the frameworks of both local and world culture. Kazakhs, as bearers of the knowledge of their own heritage, and once again entering into the arena of world history, are worthy of the interest and attention of the world's mainstream cultures. Kazakhs can enter into the modern, global cultural dialogue as equals. This book, appearing simultaneously in three languages, is intended from the outset for three large groups of readers: Kazakh-speakers, Russian-speakers, and English-speakers. Thus it is intended for representatives of three cultural worlds, three great civilizations, and it has something to say here and now for all three: For Kazakhs, this work is a reminder of the greatness, wisdom and beauty of their own traditions; for Russians, it is a reminder of the nobility, artistry and courage of their eternal neighbors throughout Eurasia; and for the Western world it is a reminder of the deep historical roots, the original philosophy of daily life and the remarkable historical experience of the nomadic civilization that it does not yet know well, a civilization that has always been an integral part of world culture, and without which, our world becomes more impoverished.

Cultures look upon one another as through a mirror, which brings them to life. Behold then, the familiar and unfamiliar aspects of the Kazakhs; behold, consider, and ponder, and you will comprehend a great deal not only about the Kazakhs, but about yourself as well.

*A. Kunanbay.*

Alma Kunanbay

To my parents-in-law, Wayne and Reba Foster, whose love was a constant source
of encouragement and support throughout this project.

— W.E.

To the memory of my grandmother and everpresent coauthor, Kulbarshin.

— A.K.

THE SACRED MOUNTAIN KHAN-TENGRI IS KNOWN AS "THE PRINCE OF SPIRITS." KAZAKHS REVERE THIS PEAK AS A SYMBOL
OF THEIR ANCIENT TENGRI FAITH, WHICH LOOKS TO THE SKY AS THE SOURCE OF THE GREAT SPIRIT. IT IS THE HIGHEST PEAK
IN KAZAKHSTAN AND THE CROWN JEWEL OF THE TIEN SHAN RANGE, WHICH ARE CALLED THE CELESTIAL MOUNTAINS.
THE UPPER THIRD OF THE MOUNTAIN IS MARBLE THAT GLOWS RED AT SUNRISE AND SUNSET.

## MOTHER EARTH: THE LAND AND THE SOUL AS ONE

The sweep of Kazakhstan takes the breath away, even if you've lived with it all your life. When confronted with these vistas for the first time, many visitors describe the experience as exhilarating. The land and its features are monumental in scale. From mountain heights to endless steppes, it is this monumentality and vastness that has forged the Kazakhs' nomadic character and spirit as well as their art and culture.

The art and culture of a nomadic society are not just art and culture in their contemporary meanings. Rather they are the very means that assure preservation of the fabric of the nomadic society.

To comprehend that art it is necessary to recognize the specific characteristics of the traditional culture as a whole. If it is true that a land and its people are inseparable and if it is true that nature determines nearly all aspects of a person's culture – from the type of economy that develops, to dwellings, clothing and food, and even to the character of the people who inhabit it – then those axioms are especially true in a nomadic society.

To understand a country means to comprehend it as an organic whole; thus, in order to *feel* its very soul, you cannot divorce the soul from the land. Given that, it would be difficult to find a better way for an initial encounter with the soul of Kazakhstan than through these rich and insightful photographic essays.

One glance at the physical map of Kazakhstan on page 13, or at the photographs herein, is enough to understand one essential point about the geography of this Central Asian country: how enormous it is. Kazakhstan occupies an area more than half the size of all of Europe. It stretches about 3,000 kilometers (1,875 miles) from the Altai Mountains in the east to the Caspian Sea in the west, and about 2,000 kilometers (1,250 miles) from the southern Ural Mountains in the north to the Tien Shan Mountains in the south. It covers more than 2.7 million square kilometers (1.04 million square miles). For its size, its population is sparse: 16.8 million, roughly 50 percent of whom are ethnic Kazakhs and 35 percent Russian; the balance are German, Ukrainian, Uzbek, Tatar, Korean, Uighur and a variety of other ethnic groups.

This sprawling landscape is fantastically diverse. It includes almost every geographic feature known to humankind except an exit onto the open sea. Kazakh territory extends all the way into the southern part of the huge West Siberian depression; and most importantly, this diverse geography determines the country's natural conditions and thereby its economy and culture.

The dominant theme in the geography is not Kazakhstan's soaring mountains or plunging valleys, not its rich forests or dappled lakes, not its broad rivers or arid deserts; it is the all-important, all-encompassing steppes. The steppe zone stretches over 2,200 kilometers (1,375 miles) from the northern part of the Caspian depression to the foothills of the Altai Mountains. The steppes are at times dusty and dry, at times snow- and ice-covered, then suddenly fragrant and full of the enchanting sounds and colors of spring. The steppe, which at a fleeting glance seems empty, constitutes a truly unique symbiosis of plant, animal and human life. The steppe demands contemplation, feeling and acclimation; then it opens up to you and gives you strength, and does not let go. To a Kazakh, the symbols of the steppe are the aroma of wormwood and steppe-grasses. According to the legend of the Polovtsians, medieval ancestors of the Kazakhs, it was the fragrance of dried wormwood that Sirchan Han, an 11th century nomad, used to tantalize his brother Otrok to return home to his native steppes.

The steppe is especially wonderful in the spring. Its boundless expanses smile with the freshness of green vegetation. The air is light and fragrant. No less than six species of larks animate the steppe from morning to evening with their songs – one moment high up in the sky, another moment flying close to the earth, then suddenly on the ground itself. Swallows and steppe hen-harriers swoop all around; an ambler bird (*zhorgha* in Kazakh) walks past; a bustard (*duadaq*) struts with its tail raised like a fan; ducks (*üyrek*) splash through the water; a cuckoo (*kökek*) hovers in the air, looking for prey on the ground where various kinds of beetles crawl, lizards leap and multicolored grasshoppers caper. On a long stalk of wild asparagus, a green grasshopper (*kök shegirtke*) extends one of its forward legs. Kazakhs say that when someone loses their way, it is enough to find this grasshopper whose extended leg will point in the right direction.

In the grassy marshes, ruffs play, and the rivers of the steppe teem with pike (*shortan*), perch (*alabugha*), sheatfish (*zhayïn*) and carp (*tuqï* and *sazan*), while the lakes are alive with tench (*qara balïq*), crucian carp (*taban*), water tortoises (*su tasbaqa*), and crayfish (*rak*). There is an almost infinite variety in the life forms along the waterways: the valleys of the Syr Darya, Irtysh, Tobol, Ishim and Ural rivers, Semirechye; or the Seven Rivers area (Zhetysu in Kazakh), and the lake districts of the Aral Sea; Kazakhstan has several thousand lakes, many of which are less than a square kilometer in area.

GOLDEN EAGLE (BÜRKIT)

Nearer to the mountains, the nightingale (*bulbul*) sings, the eagle (*bürkit*) makes its nest, the fox (*tülki*) and wolf (*qasqïr*) hunt for ducks and hares (*qoyan*), while people hunt for deer (*aq böken*) and wild ass (*qulan*). In the steppes, wind sweeps the sand dunes clean of snow even when the rest of the steppe is covered with a thick white blanket; but the dunes are so large that they conserve an enormous amount of wetness, and even in the summer it seems you can almost wring the moisture out of them when you dig.

At night the steppe appears to be even more boundless, with the blue-black sky sprinkled with myriad bright stars. Each sound carries for a great distance, be it the cry of a camel or the neigh of a horse.

Life on the steppe with its sharp seasonal and diurnal temperature changes between summer and winter and midday and dead of night has hardened Kazakhs and inured them to extremes of hot and cold. In northeastern Kazakhstan, for example, the difference in mean temperature between January and July exceeds 41 degrees Celsius (74 degrees Fahrenheit).

For the nomad, hardiness is an unavoidable necessity of life. As soon as snow begins to melt, Kazakhs start the annual migration with their herds. Such seasonal migrations are carried out over the course of the year, usually over a range of 50 to100 kilometers (30 to 60 miles). Incredibly, there once were tribes whose migrations are known to have reached 2,000 kilometers (1,250 miles) or more over the course of a year. Each clan follows the same route from year to year, stopping by the same springs and wells as their ancestors did hundreds of years earlier, and continually returning to the same place for winter pastures.

The reason is simple: Much of Kazakhstan is unsuitable for sedentary settlement because it is an arid zone similar to Mongolia, the Arabian Peninsula, or the Sahara. Situated in the center of the Eurasian land mass far removed from all oceans, about 40 percent of the territory of Kazakhstan is desert with an annual precipitation of 8 to 18 centimeters (3.3 to 7.5 inches); about 20 percent is semi-desert; 20 percent is steppe; and only 7 percent is mixed forest-steppe. Drought is a constant feature of life.

Another significant geographical feature is its elevated territories such as the Ustyurt,

Turgay, Emba, and Betpak-Dala plateaus and the picturesque mountain systems of the Altai, Saur-Tarbagatay, Dzhungar Alatau and Trans-Ili Alatau and other western spurs of the Tien Shan with their snow-capped ridges and peaks and many mountain rivers and lakes

Thus, despite the abundance of wide-open spaces, only rarely does Kazakhstan offer completely flat or monotonous landscapes. There is always something for the eye to rest on. Mountains, elevations, even mounds serve as important coordinates – points of recognition along the way that are brought to life in Kazakh legends. The apparently inaccessible beauty of the Oqzhetpes Mountains rising from the pearly surface of Lake Burabay, or the perpetually snow-capped ridges of revered Khan-Tengri in the Tien Shan Mountains, which supply life-giving waters, are described in most songs. Khan-Tengri, which rises 6,995 meters (22,949 feet), is only about a mile lower than Mount Everest. The Tien Shan range is known as the Celestial Mountains, not without good reason.

A legend about Mount Qazygurt in southern Kazakhstan relates that, following the Great Flood, Noah's Ark came to rest on its summit and that one of his sons settled nearby. Thus the Biblical legend was overlaid upon the cult that venerates mountains, a cult in which the mythological image of the life-giving mountain is depicted as the center of the world.

Kazakhstan has been inhabited since ancient times by nomads and livestock breeders. Traditionally, the areas of the country in which the nomadic lifestyle was the norm included the Turan and Caspian depressions, the Balkhash plain, and the rolling hills as well as the plateaus of Central Kazakhstan. Up until the early 20th century, most Kazakhs were nomadic. Today the majority of Kazakhs live a sedentary or urbanized life, but in rural areas, livestock breeders often still live as nomads.

The nomadic herding lifestyle (primarily based on breeding and driving sheep, camels, and horses) was the inevitable livelihood given the scarcity of food and the harsh climate with little precipitation or other water resources. (The Aral Sea and Lake Balkhash are the two major reserves of water in the republic, though the drying up of the Aral Sea has become a major ecological catastrophe after years of chronic mismanagement and unstemmed pollution under the Soviets. Steps are now being taken to correct these conditions.)

Nomadic life on the steppes of Central Asia – including Kazakhstan – is an ancient phenomenon. Scholars believe it originated at the end of the 2nd or the beginning of the 1st millennium B.C. Today almost 190 million hectares (470 million acres), or about 85 percent of all of the agricultural land in Kazakhstan, are still used as pasturage or for raising hay. Generally, the minimum require-ments for pastoral lands for raising a sheep are 5 to 7 hectares (12 to 17 acres) in the steppe zone and 12 to 24 hectares (30 to 59 acres) in the deserts and semi-deserts of Kazakhstan. It is worth noting that in the arid zone of Eurasia the seasonal migration of wild animals – deer, wild ass, wild horses and camels – is in many ways analogous to the transit of nomads. One theory suggests that

cattle-herding peoples who once lived predominantly by hunting began to migrate in pursuit of the animals they hunted, creating an ecological niche that eventually favored relying on domesticated animals and traveling with them along the same migration routes that wild animals used as pasturage.

The symbol of Kazakh nomadic life is the horse, whose praise is sung in songs, epic tales, and stories. The winged flying horse, Tülpar, like Pegasus of the ancient Greeks, appears as a beloved character in legends and is a subject for poetic inspiration. Even today in Kazakhstan wild asses and a few of the original wild horses roam the boundless steppe. Over the years, breeds of horses were developed based on their suitability for lengthy migrations. Horses became central to nomadic life due to their endurance, their herd instinct and their ability to paw up sustenance from beneath the snow cover. At the same time, horses need plentiful water and food, require a large pasturage, reach sexual maturity between five and six years of age, and have a gestation period of about one year. Because of these limitations, according to Prof. Nurbulat Masanov, "the separate weight of the horse in the structure of the herd usually did not exceed 13 percent of the headcount of the entire herd." The predominant animals were sheep, which usually constituted about 60 percent of the entire headcount. Sheep provided the nomad with meat and milk for food, and wool for clothing and dwellings.

Indispensable in this arid climate is the proud and majestic camel, the "ship of the desert." Camels possess great stamina.

BACTRIAN CAMELS

They can travel for 10 days without water or food. Excellent pack animals, they also provide meat, milk and wool. On average, camels usually constituted about 4 percent of the headcount of the herd, though in parts of western Kazakhstan their ratio was three times higher. Goats usually constituted about 10 percent of the herd, while horned cattle (basically cows) made up about 12 percent. In the north and in mountainous regions, Kazakhs also bred yaks, which are best suited for the conditions of life high in the mountains.

The very low fertility of the soil did not allow nomads and their herds to stay in a single area for a lengthy period of time. In the worst cases, the nutrients would have been so depleted and the earth so trampled down that overgrazed land would have become infertile for many years. It was therefore vital for the nomads to know down to the exact day when, and in which direction, it was necessary to drive the animals on to new pasturage and allow the old to rest until the next year. Migrations with livestock were thus necessary for survival. Natural conditions shaped the patterns of migration. Two forms were common: meridional transhumance (which means migrating from north to south and back); and in mountain-ous regions, vertical transhumance (migrating from foothills to higher elevations and back). A third form of migration was limited to desert areas: a radial migration around sources of water, either natural or man-made. The routes were sharply delineated since wells belonged to one or another tribe and were to be used in a strictly ordered sequence.

Use of pastures also followed a strict pattern according to the time of year: Winter pastures (*qistau*) were situated predominantly in the south of Kazakhstan where there were stationary residences, a limited supply of food, and a favorable location sheltered from the wind. These homesteads were scattered some distance apart since forage was too sparse to support high concentrations of livestock. Winter was the bleakest time of year for the nomad, a time of fierce struggle for survival, a time for waiting. In early spring, as soon as it was possible, they drove their cattle to the spring pastures (*kökteu*) where the animals gave birth, and sheep had their spring dip and were shorn. This was a time of hope and the beginning of the new cycle of life. This was when people celebrated the New Year, or Naurïz. Shortly thereafter, the nomads drove their animals on to the summer pastures (*zhaylau*) and their happiest time of the year: a period when animals fattened, a time of abundant food, a time when relatives and friends met as the paths of migrations crossed. Yet even as youth played games and took holidays, preparations for the upcoming winter began once again: sewing clothing, weaving rugs and beating felt into heavy fabric. With the onset of the first cool days people left for the fall

pastures (*küzeu*), where they sheared their sheep and camels and prepared milk and meat for the trek to their winter quarters. This nomadic cycle – renewed from year to year – was not and could not be exactly the same each year, just as the seasons of successive years are not identical. What remained constant was the sensation of the natural rhythm of movement, the stability of the social organization and the relationships between people.

Taken as a whole, the nomad's way of life is quite special. It is a civilization that is unique unto itself, with its own laws governing the organization of time and space. It was vital to the nomads that they sensitively follow the cycles of nature – as it says in one song, "we are in continual pursuit of the eternal spring." The primacy of movement is the foundation of their entire worldview. Everything that is above moves: the sun and the moon, the birds and the animals. Movement becomes synonymous with life.

The success of the nomad depends upon mastery of a vast body of knowledge amassed over centuries and passed from father to son and mother to daughter. This knowledge embraces an entire complex of moral norms and work habits. Its inconceivable range can be demonstrated through one fact – the existence of no less than 300 breeds of horse, differentiated through their coloring, character, economic quality, gait and so on.

The Kazakh memory preserves thousands of sounds, colors and aromas – the smell of smoke rising from the hearth in a yurt, flatbread fried in fat, the odor of felt and fluffy hides warming up in the cold night, the fragrance of

steppe grasses and delicate wild tulips and irises in the spring, the bitter dust of autumn, and the fresh snow and crisp air of winter – a symphony of aromas that cumulatively gives rise in the Kazakh mind to an image of the homeland.

TULIP IN CHARYN CANYON

FEATHER GRASSES

Horticulturists believe that the apple was first cultivated in Kazakhstan, and today some of the world's best apples are grown there. In spurs of the Trans-Ili Alatau Mountains there grows an apple called *aport* – a unique variety the size of the head of a newborn baby, with a honey-like taste and a penetrating fragrance. Apples picked late in the fall are so plump with juices that they are practically transparent; they keep until the depths of winter and permeate the air with their aroma.

Almaty, the old capital of Kazakhstan, is named for its nearby apple orchards, and in Russian, *Almaty* means "Father Apple." (The new government moved the capital to the more centrally located city of Astana in 1998.) To natives of the area, the scent of Almaty's orchards often symbolize the homeland itself. For natives of other southern regions, an image of homeland might be summed up by the scent of melons dripping with sweetness, unlimited in variety of size, color and taste. One kind, *torlama*, has a dark-green skin with a white-webbed pattern and a crunchy interior of dark-orange pulp. These melons are often wrapped in felt and hung inside the yurt, a traditional dwelling, so that the fruit's sharp, spicy odor brings back memories of those places where the eyesight, the hearing and the sense of smell received their first lessons in the never-ending variety of life's experiences.

The fragile ecological balance of the steppe is depicted in a legend about hunting. It says that a hunter was once born into a tribe who was so skillful he could feed all of his kinfolk with the meat from his kills on the steppes. His kinsmen sang his praise, and he so loved the sound that he brought home ever larger quantities of game. It was said that he had an insatiable craving for praise. Then one day, while hunting a herd of wild asses, he developed an unquenchable thirst for blood and began to indiscriminately hunt everything alive. His friends, who did not know how to stop him, left in horror while he kept on violently and savagely killing, killing, killing. Unexpectedly he spied the lame white dame of a mountain goat. The hunter took

off in pursuit, convinced of an easy kill, but the she-goat dodged his arrows and climbed higher and higher into the mountains leading the hunter behind her. Suddenly she vanished, and the hunter found himself at the summit of a barren mountain covered with ice where, starving and frightened, he soon perished in despair. The people of his tribe were scattered across the world, and to this day this place remains devoid of animals. The moral of this legend reminds us how defenseless humans are against flattery, and how, sooner or later, nature punishes not just the individual who violates the natural order, but his entire tribe as well.

There are many such tales and legends about the life of the nomad in the great world, whose rules human beings must recognize, accept and follow in order to live in harmony with nature. Kazakhs refer to the earth as "Mother Provider" (*Ana-Zher-Ana*). The space surrounding the nomad is not perceived to be hostile. He does not fight with it, but lives within its embrace. All the elements of this world are alive: Each mountain has its legend; each well taps the bosom of Mother Earth and reminds us of the people who dug it; and every migration route is full of memories of the many generations that came that way before us.

Kazakhs are well known for their love of history – mainly oral history, which is free of ideology and the subjectivity of the persons retelling it. In the oral tradition, history appears not only in the form of legend with concentrations of folk wisdom, but also in the form of genealogy.

Detailed knowledge of genealogy – knowing one's ancestors

back seven generations, and the proscription against marrying any relatives among them – are not just a characteristic feature of exogamy; it is also an instrument for the social organization of people living in a vast territory. It is enough to note that the average population density of Kazakhstan was still about 0.5 to 2.0 persons per square kilometer in the late-19th and early-20th centuries. With such a rarefied population, the steppes of Eurasia appeared to be virtually deserted, uninhabited; but even then, people had completely domesticated this territory and it was essentially their *lebensraum*. According to the genealogies, practically everyone in the steppes is connected either by blood or marital ties. Kinship terminology among the Kazakhs may be one of the most detailed systems that has been worked out in the entire world. Mutual relations between people belonging to different tribes is determined by their position vis-à-vis one another, which has taken shape over many centuries. Even one's place at the holiday table – the *dastarqan* – and the proper order for expressing one's view during any sort of discussion are determined by one's tribal position. Genealogies include not only hundreds of individual names, geographic names and dates, but vital stories characterizing these peoples and their mutual relations. Genealogies truthfully relate peoples' victories and defeats, their virtues and flaws, and thereby allow us to feel the distant past. One of the important conceptions of the relationship among past, present and future is that each person born among a people has – theoretically speaking – the potential capacity to recall the memories of his ancestors, while at the same time representing the first link in an unbroken chain with generations yet to be. Consequently, every person in the present is a bearer of the past and the future, as though both were rolled up into one. Oral history, legends and epics not only depict the past, they also lead into the future, giving birth to a sense of participation with eternity.

Contact with the land and a dependence upon it have given the Kazakhs a very restrained and philosophical character. The memory of the rise and fall of great cultures and the fleeting nature of human life are illustrated in the expression, "Arrows are enough to fell any hero, and one *zhüt* is enough to destroy any wealth." *Zhüt* is the worst calamity that can befall a nomad. It occurs when a brief thaw is followed by an unexpected freeze that covers the pasturage with a sheet of ice and makes it impossible for weak sheep or even strong horses to forage on. During episodes of *zhüt*, a nomad's entire herd can die within a week. Another Kazakh aphorism says, "Wealth is dirt on your hands that can easily be washed away." This reminds us that human beings come into this world and leave it naked.

Life in extreme conditions demands qualities such as honesty, reliability, a love of hard work and generosity. The generous hospitality of Kazakhs is legendary and is described in consistently glowing terms in the writing of all travelers. According to the Kazakh tradition of Tengrism, the sky gives each person not only life, but also the sustenance for life, and this share is to be found wherever one is fated to be. If a guest appears at your threshold, it means that his share is being kept in your home and that you must hand it over. If you are greedy and conceal his share, it will either spoil, be destroyed or otherwise be lost. This applies to food, clothing and time that you give to a guest. This is why visitors are called *Quday qonaq*, or a "guest sent by God."

Man himself is a guest in this world, and all people are guests with respect to one another. The only element that is eternal are the people, who preserve in their memory the knowledge of many generations.

In the legendary history of the Kazakhs there was a philosopher and poet named Asan Qayghi, or Asan the Sad, who spent many years looking for paradise where larks build their nests on the backs of sheep, wolves and sheep live together in peace and harmony, spring is eternal, the streams and rivers are full, and the grass is always green. In the end, after journeying to the four corners of the earth, Asan Qayghi sadly concluded that such an ideal place does not exist on this earth, but that, happily, each place has within it a small bit of this unattainable idyll, and only through nomadic life can one gather up all these bits and pieces and preserve them in memory.

Another great legendary ancestor of the Kazakhs, Qorqït Ata, decided to seek immortality after having learned that everything in this world is mortal. He saddled up his magical white camel and headed east. At the very edge of the known world he met a somber people who were digging a grave. When he asked them who it was for, they responded, "for Qorqït." He turned around and headed back west, then to the north, then back again to the south, and wherever he went he met gravediggers who were preparing his final resting place. In a desperate battle with Death he returned to his homeland along the Syr Darya River, cut down a lone willow and hollowed out from it a *qobïz* (a two-stringed, bowed musical instrument). He then slaughtered his camel, made a resonator from its neck skin, spread out the camel's hide, and sat down and began to play. He played songs of the Kazakhs known as *küys*, one more beautiful than the other, for 20 years without stopping. People streamed from near and far to hear and learn his songs. Even Death could not touch him. Only when he became convinced of his immortality and fell asleep exhausted, did Death appear in the form of a serpent and bite him. They buried him on the high bank of the Syr Darya, and today at this place, not far from the city of Qïzïlorda, there is a monument built to honor him.

Qorqït died, but his legend lives on, reminding us of the fragility of life and the immortality of art. For this reason the world of the nomads can be found and understood – more or less completely and precisely – codified through their art and legends, their genealogies and handicrafts, and speaking through their oral history as if the dead were still alive. Epic songs and instrumental *küys* capture and preserve the customs, rituals and traditions of everyday life as well as life's milestones. Listening attentively to these songs, the inheritors of this nomadic cultural legacy and sensitive observers who are their guests can share the uniqueness and the universality and appreciate the wealth and the goodness that is the soul of Kazakhstan.

ZHAYLAU, OR HIGH MOUNTAIN MEADOWS WITH ABUNDANT GRASSES, ARE THE PLACES
WHERE NOMADS SUMMER THEIR HERDS OF SHEEP AND GOATS. THIS PASTURE IS IN THE

A BIRCH GROVE OFFERS BEAUTY AND SOLITUDE NEAR SERGEYEVKA IN NORTHERN KAZAKHSTAN.

A FOREST OF TIEN SHAN FIRS STANDS TALL IN THE ZAILIISKY ALATAU MOUNTAIN SPUR NEAR ALMATY.

THIS PEAK IN THE ZAILIISKY ALATAU SPUR RISES 4,572 METERS (15,000 FEET).

FABLED SHAMBHALA IS BELIEVED TO BE NEAR MOUNT BELUKHA WHERE THE BORDERS OF KAZAKHSTAN, SIBERIA, MONGOLIA AND CHINA MEET. IT IS THE PLACE WHERE ANCIENT WISDOM IS SAID TO BE PRESERVED, A HEAVEN ON EARTH. TIBETAN LAMAS, BUDDHIST MONKS FROM INDIA, AND KAZAKH AND SIBERIAN SHAMANS HAVE REVERED THIS MOUNTAIN SINCE ANCIENT TIMES. IT RISES MORE THAN 4,500 METERS (NEARLY 15,000 FEET) IN THE ALTAI MOUNTAINS.

BEAUTIFUL DETAILS IN NATURE ARE OFTEN SOURCES OF INSPIRATION FOR KAZAKH ARTISTS, POETS, WRITERS AND MUSICIANS. THIS ICY MOUNTAIN STREAM RUNS NEAR THE VILLAGE OF SHIBER-AUL IN THE ALMARASAN VALLEY OF THE ZAILIISKY ALATAU SPUR.

FEATHER GRASSES, LIKE THESE NEAR SERGEYEVKA, HAVE GROWN FOR MILLENNIA ONLY IN THE THIN TOPSOIL OF THE STEPPES. SOME VARIETIES ARE NOW SCARCE OR ENDANGERED SPECIES. THE STEPPES WERE COVERED IN THIS IDEAL PASTURAGE PRIOR TO THE SOVIET'S MISGUIDED VIRGIN LAND RECLAMATION POLICY OF THE 1950S UNDER WHICH NEARLY 25 MILLION HECTARES (ABOUT 62 MILLION ACRES) OF NORTHERN STEPPES WERE PLOWED UP TO PLANT WHEAT.

THE ALTAI RANGE THAT RUNS ALONG KAZAKHSTAN'S NORTHEASTERN
BORDER IS NOTED FOR ITS RIVERS, WATERFALLS, SPRINGS AND
SPECTACULAR VISTAS. MOUNT BELUKHA, OFTEN SHROUDED IN CLOUDS,
HAS ITS OWN PERSONA THAT IS STEEPED IN HISTORY AND RELIGION.
IT HAS WITNESSED CHINGIS KHAN INVADING WITH 200,000
MONGOLS, AND LISTENED AS THE CHANTS, SONGS AND LAMENTS
OF SHAMANS ECHOED OFF ITS SHEER CLIFFS.

THIS VIEW FROM THE CHILIK ROAD IS OF THE ZAILIISKY
ALATAU, A SPUR OF THE TIEN SHAN RANGE.

THE SACRED MOUNTAIN KHAN-TENGRI STANDS ALONG KAZAKHSTAN'S BORDER WITH KYRGYZSTAN AND CHINA. AT 6,995 METERS (ABOUT 23,000 FEET), IT IS ONLY A FEW THOUSAND FEET LOWER THAN MOUNT EVEREST. THIS IMAGE WAS MADE THROUGH THE OPEN WINDOW OF A KAZAKH AIR FORCE HIGH-ALTITUDE HELICOPTER FLYING AT 6,700 METERS (ABOUT 22,000 FEET).

A HERDER HEADS OUT ACROSS THE OPEN, SNOW-COVERED STEPPES TO ROUND UP HIS CAMELS WEST OF THE ILI RIVER IN THE SEMIRECHYE, OR SEVEN RIVERS AREA (ZHETYSU IN KAZAKH). IT IS LATE JANUARY, 80 KILOMETERS (50 MILES) FROM THE NEAREST TOWN, AND THE TEMPERATURE IS -26 DEGREES FAHRENHEIT (-32 DEGREES CENTIGRADE).

VAST OPEN SPACES, FRAGRANT GRASSES AND HORSES WHOSE HERITAGE DATES BACK TO THE EARLIEST RECORDS OF HISTORY REPRESENT BOTH THE ALLURE AND THE LEGACY OF THE STEPPES.

KAZAKHSTAN IS DOTTED
WITH 48,000 LAKES,
MANY SMALL, LIKE THIS
MIRROR-SURFACED ONE
AT USH-KONYR NEAR
FABRICHNY.

KAZAKHSTAN HAS AN ABUNDANT AND AMAZING RANGE OF GEOGRAPHICAL FEATURES. THE DEEP GORGE OF
CHARYN CANYON RUNS FOR MILES NEAR THE SOUTHEASTERN BORDER WITH CHINA.

KAPAT SAI, OR CHALK CANYON, IS IN THE MANGHYSTAU REGION ON THE WESTERN BORDER NEAR THE CASPIAN SEA.
IT IS ONE OF THE RICHEST ARCHEOLOGICAL SITES IN CENTRAL ASIA FOR FLINT TOOLS.

THE ANCIENT SILK ROAD THAT RAN THROUGH CENTRAL ASIA AND LINKED CHINA WITH THE COUNTRIES OF THE NEAR EAST AND EUROPE HAD THREE ROUTES. A BRANCH OF ITS NORTHERN ROUTE FOLLOWED THE ILI RIVER HERE IN SOUTHEASTERN KAZAKHSTAN.

"WHILE RESEARCHING FOR THIS BOOK IN THE NEW YORK PUBLIC LIBRARY, I CAME ACROSS A LETTER NATALYA SEDOVA, LEON TROTSKY'S WIFE, WROTE HOME WHILE EXILED IN ALMATY. SHE EXCLAIMED ABOUT THE BEAUTY OF A LATE SPRING SNOW BLANKETING THE TULIPS. AS GOOD FORTUNE WOULD HAVE IT, MY APARTMENT WAS ACROSS FROM WHERE THE TROTSKYS LIVED. ON A SPRING DAY IN APRIL, I WAS TREATED TO THE SAME BEAUTIFUL SIGHT" – W.E.

THE BRILLIANT REDS OF THE POPPIES, ROSES, TULIPS AND CARNATIONS OF SPRING AND SUMMER ARE A DIRECT INFLUENCE ON THE COLOR PALETTE OF KAZAKH ART. THESE POPPIES ARE NEAR ORDABASY IN SOUTHERN KAZAKHSTAN.

SAFFRON CROCUS IS POPULARLY KNOWN AS SNOWDROPS. THIS FRAGRANT WHITE FLOWER IS ONE OF THE FIRST TO BLOOM IN FEBRUARY. THIS SHOT WAS TAKEN IN THE ZAILIISKY ALATAU AT AN ALTITUDE OF ABOUT 3,700 METERS (12,000 FEET).

A WILDFLOWER AT USH-KONYR NEAR FABRICHNY MAKES A DELICATE PORTRAIT.

SUNFLOWERS IN A FIELD
CONTRAST WITH THE HILLS
NEAR OSKEMEN IN EASTERN
KAZAKHSTAN.

SUMMER CARPETS OF WILDFLOWERS, LIKE THIS ONE NEAR FABRICHNY IN SOUTHEASTERN KAZAKHSTAN, MAKE IT EASY TO
IDENTIFY ONE OF THE INSPIRATIONS FOR DESIGNS AND COLORS IN KAZAKH RUGS AND TEXTILES. GRASSY, SUBALPINE
MEADOWS LIKE THIS ONE MAY HAVE AS MANY AS 100 SPECIES OF FLOWERS.

A MEADOW OF WILDFLOWERS OVERLOOKS THE ESIL (ISHIM) RIVER NEAR PETROPAVL IN NORTHERN KAZAKHSTAN.

BOLSHOE ALMATINSKOE
OZERO (BIG ALMATY LAKE)
IN THE ZAILIISKY ALATAU
IS GLACIER FED. IT IS A
SIGNIFICANT SOURCE OF
WATER FOR ALMATY. ITS
PURE QUALITY CAUSES THE
SURFACE TO CHANGE WITH
THE LIGHT FROM PALE TO
DARK TURQUOISE OVER
THE COURSE OF THE DAY.

BUKHTARMA RIVER VALLEY
IN THE KATON-KARAGAI AREA
IN EASTERN KAZAKHSTAN IS A
VERDANT GREEN LANDSCAPE OF
WILDFLOWERS AND WHEAT. IN
NEAT VILLAGES, EACH HOUSE
HAS AN OVERFLOWING GARDEN
TUCKED NEXT TO IT. THIS AREA
NEAR THE ALTAI MOUNTAINS
IS RENOWNED FOR THE LUSCIOUS
QUALITY OF THE HONEY IT
PRODUCES.

THE CASPIAN SEA ON KAZAKHSTAN'S WESTERN BORDER IS RICH IN OIL AND STURGEON. NOT REALLY A SEA AT ALL, IT IS THE WORLD'S LARGEST LAKE, AND THE SOURCE OF WORLD-FAMOUS BELUGA CAVIAR. THIS SCENE WAS TAKEN NEAR AKTAU IN THE MANGHYSTAU REGION.

THE TIEN SHAN MOUNTAINS ARE COVERED WITH FIRS THAT LOOK LIKE FORESTS OF CHRISTMAS TREES SUCH AS THESE
IN THE BAYANKOL RIVER VALLEY IN SOUTHEASTERN KAZAKHSTAN.

WILD APRICOT AND
BARBERRY BUSHES PAINT
THE HILLS OF THE
ZAILIISKY ALATAU IN
VIVID ORANGES AND REDS.

THE APPLE WAS FIRST DOMESTICATED IN KAZAKHSTAN. THESE "WILD APPLES," AS THEY ARE FORMALLY NAMED, GROW IN AN ANCIENT ORCHARD AT THE PANFILOVSK'Y FARM OUTSIDE ALMATY. THEY ARE BELIEVED TO BE REMNANTS OF PRIMEVAL FORESTS AND ARE CURRENTLY SUBJECTS OF APPLE GENETIC STUDIES. HORTICULTURISTS BELIEVE SEEDS AND CUTTINGS FROM THESE ORCHARDS SPREAD ON ANCIENT TRADE ROUTES TO THE MIDDLE EAST, EUROPE, AND ACROSS THE BERING STRAITS INTO NORTH AMERICA. THE NAME ALMATY TRANSLATES AS "FATHER APPLE."

## LAND OF OUR FATHERS: THE SPIRIT OF THE ANCESTORS

If Mother Earth embodies the essence of the land and the soul of the people, the "Land of Our Fathers" is the spiritual cradle in which the Kazakh people were nourished and grew.

To a Kazakh, the homeland is the territory of a people who, over several thousand years, have turned one stretch of terrain after another into their dwelling place and have created their culture upon it.

The history of civilization in Kazakhstan goes as far back as the Iron Age. The earliest finds of archeologists indicate settlements in the steppes in the Neolithic and Late Neolithic periods (8,000 to 2,000 B.C.). Stone implements from this era have been found during excavations in central and eastern Kazakhstan, as well as on the Mangyshlak Peninsula.

Basically these settlements, which were grouped along rivers, lakes and the foothills of mountains, attest to a predominantly settled way of life. The many petroglyphs found in Kazakhstan also belong to that era. Their number and quality is comparable to those from the greatest sites of the art of ancient man. Among them are depictions of sorcerers and beasts, dragons and monsters, scenes of hunts and tribal campaigns, stags, deer, horsemen, chariots, priestesses, amazons, and symbolic maps of the world that

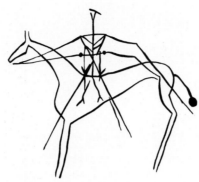

are remarkable for their expressiveness of detail.

The cosmic scenes carved in the Eshkiölmes Mountains (near the present-day city of Taldykorgan) and the Tamghalï Valley of the southern reaches of the Chu-Ili Mountains are unforgettable. The images of solar deities, for example, demonstrate the complexity and sophistication of representations by the inhabitants of this territory during the Bronze Age (2nd millennium B.C.). It is as if they created early portrayals of the dynamics of the planetary system.

According to the most recent hypothesis, the ancient population of Kazakhstan was linguistically derived from Iranian and was anthropologically Proto-Europaeoid, though traces of Mongoloid features begin to appear on this territory around the 1st millennium B.C.

By the middle of the 1st millennium B.C. some of the Central Asian tribes were already converted to a pastoral nomadic life, and soon larger unions of tribes began to appear, among them the Scytho-Sarmatian and Saka-Scythian cultural centers.

The Kazakh homeland preserves and is mindful of the history of the people who inhabited

it during the 1st millennium B.C., and some of their secrets are revealed to us through the discoveries of archeologists. Thus, in 1969 in the town of Issïq, about 50 kilometers (31 miles) from Almaty, there was an amazing discovery. In the foothills of Mount Talgar, the highest peak of the Trans-Ili Alatau Mountains, a splendidly preserved burial site from the era of the earliest nomads of the Iron Age was unearthed. This is the grave of a Saka warrior chieftain, perhaps the ruler of the Scythians, whom Prof. Alisher Akishev has dated to the 5th to 4th century B.C. This burial site is unique for its completeness and its state of preservation. All of the chieftain's apparel and finery are extant. He was dressed in a chamois tunic decorated with small golden badges embossed with the head of a tiger; tight leather britches that are laced with thongs and covered with small golden badges above high boots; a golden collar around the neck; in the left ear, an earring with a turquoise drop; and on the hands two signet rings, one with the image of the sun god.

Especially striking is the warrior's headgear: a gold, cone-shaped hat (*qulaq*) 70 centimeters (29 inches) tall, with more than 200 representations of birds, winged horses, arrows, feathers and mountains. The peak of the

conical hat is crowned with a miniature golden statue of a wild mountain ram. The warrior was entombed with his dagger in a

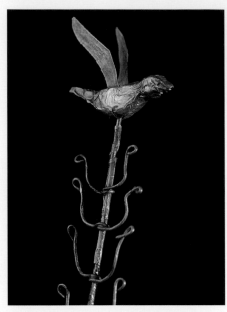

ORIGINAL TREE OF LIFE, **GOLDEN MAN** HEADDRESS

sheath on his left, a long sword decorated with animals on his right, and ceramic vessels and copper and silver cups. On the bottom of one artifact is an as yet undeciphered inscription in the "language of the Sakas" or "Issïq

ORIGINAL DEER BELT DECORATION, **GOLDEN MAN**

writing," which scholars attribute to the Iranian branch of the Indo-European language stock. Numerous items that reflect the worldview and beliefs of the

ORIGINAL CAFTAN DECORATION, **GOLDEN MAN**

early nomads of the Saka tradition were also found. A copy of this Golden Warrior, or "the Golden Man," as he popularly came to be known, toured the world in the 1990s following independence, drawing the admiration of millions of viewers. It was on view at the United Nations headquarters in New York City. Meanwhile, the symbolism of this burial site is still being discussed by specialists in a number of fields.

A significant number of the ancient caravan routes that linked China with the countries of the Near East and Europe, known today as the Silk Road, crossed the territory of Central Asia from the 3rd century B.C. all the way to the 19th century A.D. The Silk Road served as the main artery between East and West for trade that included not only silk, spices, jewels and medicinal plants, but also cultural values, technological ideas and world religions such as Buddhism, Judaism, Christianity and Islam. Together, these religions spread the writing systems of various peoples, their traditions, customs, cuisines and even their fashions. Thus in China there was a time

when Turkic clothing, music and even the yurt were fashionable at the court of the emperor.

All along the Silk Road, towns and cities developed with noisy and colorful markets where the din of dozens of different languages could be heard. Archeologists in Kazakhstan continue to discover coins, statues, vases, textiles, decorations and other artifacts that originated in India, Byzantium, Persia and China. And today among the musical instruments of the peoples of the Silk Road, the sounds of ancient Central Asian instruments can still be heard. The oldest of these, the bowed string instrument called the *qobïz*, once used by Kazakh shamans, is the ancestor of the European violin.

One of the most far-reaching phenomena in the history of civilization – comparable even to man's journeys into space – occurred in the steppes of Central Asia more than 2,000 years ago. That event was the domestication of the horse. News of this development was brought to the Chinese emperor's court by his envoy. This royal courtier, who spent 13 years among the nomads, told the emperor what he had witnessed and marveled at "the celestial horses of the nomads sweating blood."

Around the middle of the 1st millennium A.D., the movement of ancient Turks from the Altai Mountains to the west began,

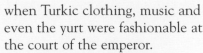

which gradually changed the ethnic and linguistic situation in Eurasia through the uninterrupted genetic succession of its population. As time passed, the anthropological type and linguistic patterns in the steppes changed. Early in the 6th century A.D., with the rise of the Turkic Empire, Turkic languages became predominant.

By the beginning of the 2nd millennium A.D., an ethnic, linguistic and cultural unity of tribes had formed on what is now Kazakhstan that appears to be a direct ancestor of today's Kazakhs. By the end of the 12th century this was already a complex civilization consisting of towns in addition to nomadic populations. The medieval towns of southern Kazakhstan such as Otrar, Sighnaq, Sauran, Sozaq and Yassï, were centers of cultural and economic life and represented an indissoluble unity with the network of nomads who functioned in a mutually dependent relationship. The invasion of Chingis Khan (known better in the West as Genghis Khan) at the beginning of the 13th century changed the political map of the region and destroyed the towns. But it did not end the process of consolidation of the steppe tribes who, in their typically steadfast fashion, readily adapted to and absorbed the newcomers and continued to persevere in their ancient homeland.

From the point of view of culture this resilience is perhaps the most remarkable phenomenon. Over the course of thousands of years, the ancient indigenous population of the steppes of Eurasia evolved, developed and survived, inheriting and incorporating the very best of the preceding epochs.

The figure of Chingis Khan, the conqueror of medieval Eurasia, is a paradox in Kazakh history. Historians know well that he practically stopped the natural development of steppe civilization by destroying its greatest urban and cultural centers including Otrar, which had a library famous throughout the medieval world as second only to the earlier one in Alexandria. Yet in folklore he is not a malevolent destroyer, but rather a full-fledged figure in the ethnic history of the Kazakhs. The steppe aristocracy traces its genealogy from the descendants of Chingis Khan, and it is only from them that the Kazakh khans could be chosen. Legends about his miraculous birth abound. Long before he became Chingis Khan, he was born as Temüjin (in Turkic, Temirshi, or "iron-smith") – whom legend says was conceived by a ray of sunshine that impregnated his mother. There are tales about the white cloud that followed and protected him; and there is the story of the tragic death of his son Jochi (Zhoshï) Khan, and the related tale of Ketbugha, the father of

music, who informed Chingis Khan of Jochi's death – all of this is an organic part of Kazakh folklore. Variations of the name Chingis (Shïngïs in Kazakh) are widely used among the peoples of Central Asia; and the name has become especially popular in our time as well, thanks to the great 20th century Central Asian writer, Chingiz Aytmatov.

One of the reasons for such tolerance of the events surrounding the Mongol invasion is that there were a large number of related Turkic tribes within the armies of Chingis Khan. For greater mobility, his armies maneuvered around the Kazakh steppes without the burdensome caravans carrying wives and children; instead, the conquerors married into the local, ethnically concentrated environment and assimilated into it. The religious tolerance in Chingis Khan's policies made it possible for the conquered peoples to preserve their beliefs and customs, which allowed the local cultures to thrive as well.

The history of Kazakhstan, taken within the framework of Central Asia as a whole, is extremely complicated in all of its periods, from the ancient to the modern. An endless recitation of names and dates, khanates and battles, conquests and defeats would say very little to a reader unfamiliar with them. Even the nomad himself does not measure history as much by a literal chronology as by a basic genealogy, i.e., the history of tribes, clans,

and family lineages. For a very general orientation of Kazakh history one needs to know a few prominent landmarks – for example, the period of Chingis Khan, the establishment of statehood, its loss first to the Russian and later to the Soviet Empires, as well as an understanding of local religious beliefs and views.

In the history of the Kazakhs there are names that are known to everyone; there are also dates that are considered ethnic watersheds. Thus, in the 15th and 16th centuries, on the ruins of the Mongol empire, the first Kazakh state emerged – the Kazakh khanate. Ruled by the khans Kerey and Zhanïbek, the khanate was proclaimed in 1456 in western Semirechye by the river Chu, on Qozi-basi Mountain. Kerey and Zhanïbek founded Kazakh statehood and unified the great number of tribes that lived similar lifestyles and had close cultural contacts over many centuries. What made this state unique was its nomadic aspects and its social structure.

Early Kazakh society was organized according to a tripartite principle and was separated into three hordes: the Great Horde, Middle Horde and Lesser Horde (Ulï Zhüz, Orta Zhüz, and Kishi Zhüz). The hordes also had territorial demarcations: the Great Horde dominated southern and eastern Kazakhstan; the Middle Horde, central Kazakhstan; and the Lesser Horde, western Kazakhstan. The hordes were

divided further into tribes and clans.

The division of society by *zhüz* is integral to the long history of the formation of the Kazakh state and its many-sided contacts with tribes such as the Uysun, Arghïn and Aday. This division had socioeconomic as well as geographic aspects. A proverb states: "Give the Great Horde a staff in its hands and place it over the herd; give the Middle Horde a pen in its hand and send it to a dispute; give the Lesser Horde a pike in its hand and send it into battle." This proverb highlights the sociological differentiation of the Kazakh people – a division into rulers, priests, and warriors that reflects the dominant activities of each *zhüz* without becoming a strictly defined caste system as in India. These dominant themes of the early Kazakh hordes also put their stamp on how each region evolved: A complex economy guaranteeing the wealth of the entire people emerged in the south; central Kazakhstan came

to be known for the astute political activities of its representatives; and western Kazakhstan was marked by endless wars to determine boundaries.

Underlying the territorial and socioeconomic tripartite system of the *zhüz*, the notion of a vertical division is deeply rooted in Kazakh folklore. There are, for example, the countless stories of the three brothers, a universal motif that reflects the differences between the three hordes. The tripartite character of the hordes' structure is deeply ingrained not only in daily life, but in the entire philosophical system of the Kazakh worldview. Because each *zhüz* was headed by its own khan, a list of those names is also the story of the flow of Kazakh history.

A khan was named through democratic principles from the ranks of the most talented warriors and politicians. Selection culminated with an installation ritual in which the khan was seated on a white felt rug that represented justice and the pure and holy Upper World. The khan would be raised skyward on the felt three times by tribal leaders. The khan did not have autocratic powers since disagreement with his policies could result in an outward migration of his tribes to neighboring territories. And the khan, while symbolizing the highest authority, was not considered "God's representative on earth" – within the khan's residence, for example, it was enough for his subjects to nod with their heads rather than to prostrate themselves on their knees as a sign of respect. Under this system of government an important role was played by the khan's advisers, who skillfully exercised authority through eloquent speech and the art of debate. The advisers of the khans were epic singers – connoisseurs of ancient and contemporary history.

From this time on, the ethnic designation Qazaq is encountered in European, Russian, Persian, Chinese and Armenian texts, as well as in Chaghatay, a Central Asian, Turkic-Arabic script also used in the khanate. But the cultural history of the Kazakhs is much older than its political history. The exact origins of the ethnonym *Kazakh* are still shrouded in mystery and are the subject of many hypotheses and much scholarly debate.

Legends and mythology about the origins of the "Kazakh" people abound. One of them is as follows: During a time of terrible wars long ago an entire settlement and its inhabitants were destroyed. Only one newborn male infant, hidden in his cradle, survived. A female wolf heard his cries and saved the boy. She brought him home to her lair and fed him and raised him. This child was the ancestor of the Kazakhs.

Thus, it is no coincidence that the flag of the Shapïrashtï tribe of the Kazakh Great Horde depicts a wolf's head. In other versions the wolf motif can take the form of the sheep dog or the hunting dog, particularly in Kazakh rituals regarding children. The tooth or claw of a wolf are

often used as amulets, and a wolf's hide is placed in the most honored place in nearly every Kazakh's yurt to protect its inhabitants. Venerating the wolf as a totem animal and not as an irreconcilable enemy, is one of the elements that resolves philosophically the contradiction between the world of the steppe and the life of the pastoralist. This particular trait – knowing how to accept life with all of its difficulties and to include, assimilate and absorb rather than to exclude, oppose and destroy – is one of the characteristics of the wise and philosophical worldview of the Kazakhs.

Another legend ties the genealogy of the Kazakhs to the Biblical Noah, whose Ark is said to have come to rest upon the summit of Mount Qazygurt in southern Kazakhstan. According to this story, Kazakhs are descended from Noah's middle son (named Sam in the Kazakh version). A third legend relates that an ancestor of the Kazakhs named Alash was born with a variety of unusual markings. Fearful that the birth of an heir so marked

was a bad sign, his tribe placed him in a trunk and threw it into the sea. A poor shepherd found, rescued and raised the child. And Alash's six sons grew up to become the ancestors of six related peoples: the Kazakhs, the Kyrgyz, the Kara-Kalpaks, the Nogai, the nomadic Uzbeks and the Turkmen. Even today, Kazakhs sometimes refer to themselves as "the children of the six sons of Alash." A fourth mythological story tells of an obstinate prince who went out into the open steppes with his friends where he lived the free-spirited, carefree life of a bachelor. Three times his father sent hundreds of horsemen out after him, but they, too, enjoyed the freedom of the steppes and decided to stay with the prince. Later, having taken wives from a variety of different tribes, they settled down and developed into a large community of freedom-loving people – the Kazakhs. A fifth legend connects the name Qazaq with the word *qaz,* which means "swan or goose." In this story, one of the military commanders in the steppes, Qalsha-Qadïr, was dying of hunger while separated from his troops, but he was saved by a white goose or swan (*qaz-aq*) that descended from the sky. He fell in love and married the swan, and Qalsha-Qadïr became the ancestor of all Kazakhs, whose name came to mean "people of the swan." There are other storied etymologies for the ethnonym, such as *Xas saq,* or True Saq; and *Qay saq,* or Regal Saq. But these

don't correspond to the emergence of a cultural unity and often even differ from what the people call themselves. In the Russian ethnographic literature of the 19th and early 20th centuries, for example, Kazakhs were known as Kirgiz-Kaysaki or simply Kirgizï, even though that was the name of a completely different ethnic group distantly related to the Kazakhs, and who were, in turn, mislabeled by ethnographers as Kara-Kirgizï (Black Kyrgyz) or as Dikokamennïe-Kirgizï (Mountain Kyrgyz). The self-appellation *Qazaq* corresponds more closely to the Russian word *Kozak*, but the latter refers to inhabitants of military settlements on the southern frontiers of the Russian Empire.

However confusing this array of names and etymologies and the abundance of legends and hypotheses about the origins of the Kazakh people may be, it cannot hide the most important point – namely, the unity of Kazakh ethnic identity over the course of centuries. And the 15th to 18th centuries are known as their heroic period. It was an era lauded in epic poetry that is filled with unique characters and fascinating conflicts and challenges – truly an era of knights. It called attention to the beauty and richness of nomadic civilization. During this time ethnic awareness formed and solidified during countless campaigns for independence. It was the beginning of the Kazakhs' journey on a long road of trials and tribulations.

The greatest struggle for survival was the war against the invading Dzungars (or Oyrat Mongols), who were from Dzungaria in what is now northwestern China. The Dzungar Khanate, established in 1635, was from its outset the greatest threat from the East. For an entire century wars raged between the Kazakh and Oyrat tribes in a pendulum of frequent swings between victory and defeat. In the 17th and 18th centuries the Dzungars conquered a vast territory inhabited by Kazakhs and destroyed towns such as Sayram, Turkestan, and Tashkent. The Kazakh people preserve memories of the most difficult pages from these wars, one of which – the Years of the Great Impoverishment – occurred between 1723 and 1725. It was the destruction of Dzungaria during the next quarter century by the Ch'ing dynasty in China that, for all practical purposes, saved the Kazakhs from genocide. Between 1465 and 1723, the Kazakh population had grown from about 1.1 million to 3.3 million, but during the Years of the Great Impoverishment, about a third of their people died.

The conflicts with the Dzungars found an artistic embodiment in the well-known epic poems of both peoples; it also brought outstanding Kazakh figures onto the historical stage, such as Abulkhayr Khan of the Lesser Horde and Abïlay Khan of the Middle Horde. In the 1730s and 1740s they made the first agreements between the Kazakh

hordes and Russia, a political and military power that – so it seemed to them – could serve as a bulwark in the exhausting, century-long battle to preserve their independence. Ironically, it also opened the door to eventual imperial colonization, a period that would prove to be no less or no more contradictory for Kazakhs than all the preceding periods had been.

It is worth noting here that women also played an important role in the fight to preserve independence during those long years. Kazakh epics tell of brave "Amazons" who were faithful friends and counselors to the male heroes. They fought for independence side by side, and led their tribes during the men's absence. History has preserved the names of women such as Gauhar-qïz, wife of Qarakerey Qabanbay, who led an army in the war against the Oyrat Mongols in the 18th century, and Bopay, sister of Kenesarï, who fought against Russian colonization in the 19th century. And during the Great Patriotic War, as World War II is known, the names of brave daughters of the Kazakh people such as Manshuq Mametova and Aliya Moldagulova, who died heroically, have entered into the annals of history and represent in their own way a continuation of the epic history of the Kazakhs.

In any case, the policies of the Russian Empire regarding Kazakhstan were from the very start colonial in nature. The great

natural wealth of raw materials in the region; the tremendous ready market for Russian manufactured goods; "empty" territories for expansion; the only suitable passage to the wealth of Samarkand, Bukhara and farther on to the India of legend – all of these goals first required the subjugation of the steppe. All of Russia's military, diplomatic and scholarly resources of the time were brought to bear in single-minded fashion. Notwithstanding the impatience of Imperial Russia to absorb the steppe, it took 150 years to achieve this ambitious goal. The tsarist colonial policy was continued and refined by Bolshevik Russia. Kazakhs paid an immeasurably high price in order to survive the century of colonial rule until they achieved independence again in 1991.

The Soviet expansion was a struggle not just for territory, but for the hearts and minds of the people who lived there. Armed with the concept of European superiority and its "civilizing" mission, the Soviets saw in the nomads a bastardized and illiterate band of barbarians who were only capable of destruction and who had no rights. The forcible transformation or even the elimination of the nomads was seen by the Soviets as a blessing

for future generations. As a result, the people of Kazakhstan – the heirs of a 3,000-year-old nomadic civilization – lost 70 percent of their population during the first decade of Soviet rule through sedentarization, famine, repression and emigration. Only in 1976 did the ethnic Kazakh population regain the level of 5.6 million recorded during the 1916 census. Due to a consistent policy of forced resettlement of Slavic and other ethnic groups to steppe territories, Kazakhs as a percentage of the population within their own homeland fell from 75 percent in 1900 to 29.8 percent in 1959.

Today Russians, Ukrainians, Belorussians, Poles, Germans, Chechens, Koreans and representatives of almost 100 other ethnic groups live in Kazakhstan in addition to the republic's indigenous population. According to 1991 statistics, the world population of ethnic Kazakhs numbers about 10 million. Of these, about 6.8 million live in Kazakhstan; 1.7 million live in the other republics of the former Soviet Union; and 5.5 million live in other countries. The number of indigenous Kazakhs within the Republic of Kazakhstan became a majority once again only in 1997.

On the conscience of the Communist regime, omitting mention of many other wrongs, are a number of dire offenses with tragic results. One of the most egregious was the use of the Semipalatinsk area in northeastern Kazakhstan as a nuclear testing ground. From 1949 to 1989 about 500 nuclear explosions

were conducted in populated areas, resulting in the sickness or death of thousands of people and a landscape that became an uninhabitable wasteland. Another disaster was Soviet Premier Nikita Khrushchev's "virgin lands" campaign that resulted in massive erosion of topsoil on lands not suited for agriculture. A third tragedy is the drying up of the vast Aral Sea, an ecological catastrophe caused by excessive diversion of the waters from the Amu Darya and Syr Darya Rivers for irrigation of cotton. The Soviets called cotton the "white gold" of Central Asia, and the state received truly golden prices for it on the world market. And there is more, much more that still pains the soul of Kazakhstan today. But the Kazakh soul is not defeated – it is only hardened and made stronger by its struggles. And in this endless chain of suffering she is aided by her spiritual underpinnings that are embodied in the culture of the people.

Fairness demands acknowledgment that the 70 years of Soviet rule were not just a time of defeats, but of great accomplishments as well. In response to the effort to completely deprive the people of their mother tongue and to turn them solely into Russian speakers, Kazakhs instead became

possible not only for study but for creativity in both languages. This cultural bilingualism enabled Kazakhs to make a natural shift to the study of other world languages, and students from Kazakhstan now

among the sedentary population (in Semirechye and along the Syr Darya River). By the 12th century Islam had spread generally, and today the majority of Kazakhs are Muslims of the Hanafi legal school. In southern Kazakhstan Sufism is

Creator; and the protectress of fertility and mothers, named Umay. Islam also coexists with shamanism (*baqsïlïq*), represented by the figure of Baqsï, a musician, healer and soothsayer. *Baqsïlïq* had a fundamental impact upon

THIS HORSE WITHIN A HORSE AT TAMGHALÏ IS A UNIQUE PETROGLYPH.

work or research at practically every great university of the world.

In response to the Soviets' appalling effort to convert Kazakhs to atheism, Kazakhs persevered and in one measure or another preserved the layers of their religious history from shamanism to Zoroastrianism, and from Tengrism to Islam.

Islam was brought by Arabs to Central Asia in the 6th to 8th centuries, and by the end of the 10th century it had established itself on the southern territory of present-day Kazakhstan first

also well known. It is connected with the descendants of Hodja Akhmed Yasavi (circa 1103 to 1166), and the city of Turkestan, where he died, which is located in present-day Kazakhstan, and is considered by Muslim Turks to be a lesser Mecca.

The oldest religion of the nomads, Tengrism, also exists among the Kazakhs, often in combination with Islam. Tengrism involves the worship of the sky deity named Tengri, the male Creator; the earth-water deity called Zher-Suw, the female

all aspects of the traditional culture and art of the Kazakhs.

A close relationship with nature, a responsiveness to all its influences, and veneration of mountains, caves, rivers and lakes still coexists with other religious practices among many Kazakhs. Veneration of fire can also be found in many rites and rituals, in which some see the heritage of Zoroastrianism and the cult of ancestors and the images of Sufi poetry all brightly burning.

THIS PANEL, CALLED "PANTHEON OF SUN GODS" BY ARCHEOLOGISTS, IS ONE OF MORE THAN 2,000 PETROGLYPHS AT TAMGHALÏ CREATED
BETWEEN THE BRONZE AGE AND THE RENAISSANCE. PETROGLYPHS ON FIVE LARGE ROCK FACES CAN BE VIEWED AS ONE FROM A NEARBY
CEREMONIAL SITE AS THE SETTING SUN ILLUMINATES THEM. THIS DETAIL DESCRIBES THE KAZAKH FAITH CALLED TENGRI. THE ONE HORIZONTAL
PERSON ON THE BOTTOM LEFT REPRESENTS MOTHER EARTH FROM WHOM ALL LIFE ISSUES. THE LINE OF DANCING FIGURES REPRESENTS THE
PHYSICAL DIMENSION OF OUR LIVES ON EARTH. THE SUN GOD FIGURES REPRESENT THE DIMENSION OF THE GREAT SPIRIT AND OUR ANCESTORS.
THESE THREE LEVELS OF EXISTENCE ARE NOT SEPARATE, BUT EXIST CONCURRENTLY AND IN UNITY. TAMGHALÏ IS ON AN ANCIENT
NORTH-SOUTH ROUTE IN THE CHU-ILI MOUNTAINS OF SOUTHEASTERN KAZAKHSTAN.

THIS BRONZE AGE PETROGLYPH
AT TAMGHALÏ OF A SUN GOD
RIDING A BULL COMBINES THE
SYMBOL OF FERTILITY AND
THE SYMBOL OF THE SOURCE
OF LIFE.

KAZAKH LEGEND TELLS THAT ONE OF NOAH'S THREE SONS SETTLED NEAR MOUNT QAZYGURT IN SOUTHERN KAZAKHSTAN AND CREATED THIS CIRCLE OF STONES 40 METERS (131 FEET) IN DIAMETER WITH A CROSS IN THE CENTER. THERE IS A SIMILAR CIRCLE IN TURKEY AND ANOTHER IN THE SINAI PENINSULA. THE CONJECTURE IS THAT AFTER THE GREAT FLOOD, NOAH'S SONS SET OUT WITH THEIR FAMILIES, AND EACH MARKED THE PLACE THEY CHOSE TO SETTLE WITH THIS SYMBOL.

THIS PICTOGRAPH CARRIES MULTIPLE MEANINGS. ONE IS A STYLIZED FIGURE OF A DWELLING IN THE FORM OF A MAN; THE DWELLING RESEMBLES A TEEPEE. THE PICTOGRAPH IS DONE IN A TECHNIQUE CALLED **PISANITSY** USING OCHER. IT DATES TO THE ENEOLITHIC PERIOD IN KAZAKHSTAN (C. 4,000 TO 3,000 B.C.) BETWEEN THE STONE AND THE BRONZE AGES. IT WAS FOUND AT AKBAUR GROTTO IN EASTERN KAZAKHSTAN.

AKBAUR GROTTO IS INSIDE A GRANITE HILL THAT RESEMBLES A PYRAMID. A CLIMB UP 20 FEET OF NATURAL, STEP-LIKE FOLDS SYMBOLIZES STAIRS THAT CONNECT THE PHYSICAL REALM TO THE SUPERNATURAL REALM. A NATURAL OPENING IN THE GROTTO RESEMBLES THE **SHANGÏRAQ** ROOF OPENING OF A YURT. AS THE SUN MAKES ITS DAILY COURSE ACROSS THE HEAVENS, ITS RAYS ENTER THE GROTTO AND ILLUMINATE THE 80 PICTOGRAPHS DEPICTING ANCIENT KAZAKH MYTHOLOGY AND COSMOLOGY.

THIS OCHER PICTOGRAPH DEPICTS A RAM. RAMS AND MOUNTAIN GOATS HAVE BOTH BEEN USED IN MANY CULTURES OVER THE CENTURIES AS SYMBOLS FOR FERTILITY. THEY ALSO SYMBOLIZE PURITY AND A CONNECTION BETWEEN HEAVEN AND EARTH, IN PART BECAUSE THEY CLIMB SO HIGH IN THE MOUNTAINS WHERE THE AIR IS PURE. IT IS ALSO FROM THE ENEOLITHIC PERIOD AT AKBAUR GROTTO.

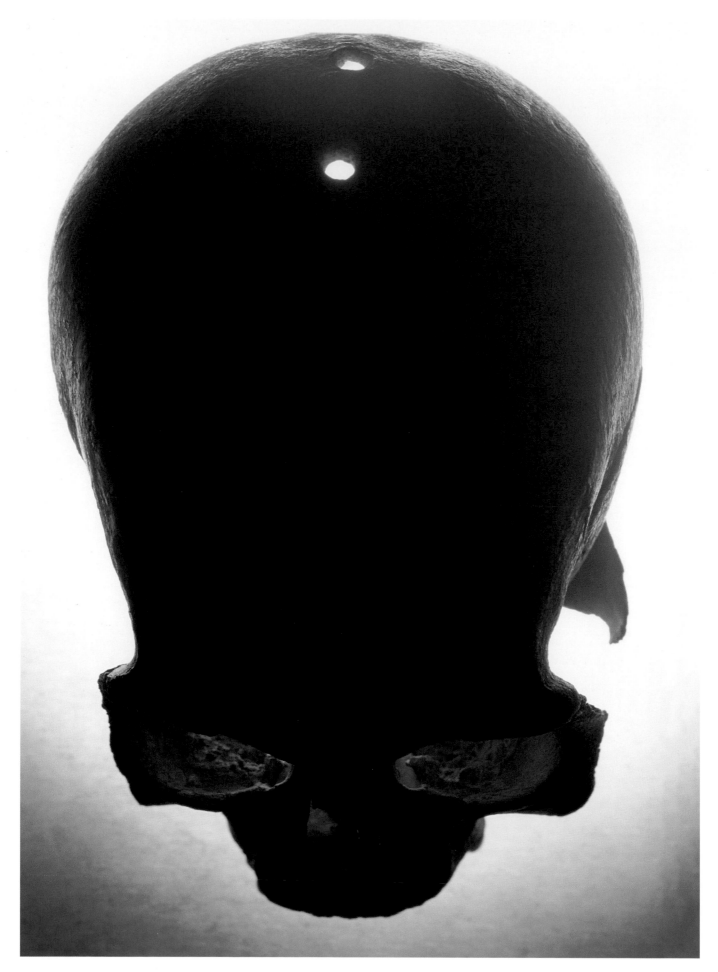

THIS 5,000-YEAR-OLD SKULL IS BELIEVED TO BE THAT OF A 30-YEAR-OLD SHAMAN. TWO HOLES WERE DRILLED IN THE SKULL WHEN THE PERSON WAS 15 YEARS OLD AND HE OR SHE LIVED ANOTHER 15 YEARS AFTER THAT. THE SKULL WAS FOUND WITH A CLAY MASK ON ITS FACE IN A NICHE IN A DWELLING IN NORTHERN KAZAKHSTAN. IT WAS DISCOVERED AT THE BOTAI SETTLEMENT SITE IN THE ATYRAUSKY DISTRICT. NORTH KAZAKHSTAN REGIONAL HISTORICAL MUSEUM, PETROPAVL.

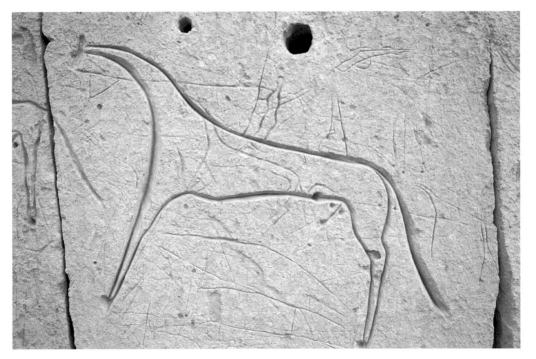

STUDIES SHOW THAT THE HORSE WAS FIRST DOMESTICATED IN KAZAKHSTAN. THIS HORSE SKULL, DISCOVERED IN THE NORTH BY PROFESSOR VICTOR ZAIBERT IN 1986, SHOWS THE WEAR OF A BRIDLE ON THE TEETH. CARBON-14 TESTING PUTS ITS AGE AT 5,000 YEARS. THOUSANDS OF ADDITIONAL ARTIFACTS FOUND OVER A 15-YEAR EXCAVATION PERIOD AT BOTAI SETTLEMENT SITE ALONG THE IMAN-BURLUK RIVER IN THE ATYRAUSKY DISTRICT FURTHER SUBSTANTIATE THIS FACT.
NORTH KAZAKHSTAN REGIONAL HISTORICAL MUSEUM, PETROPAVL.

FROM ANCIENT TIMES THROUGH THE MIDDLE AGES, PETROGLYPHS, PAINTINGS AND CARVINGS SHOW RIDERS CARRYING BANNERS – USUALLY ON HORSEBACK. DURING THE MIDDLE AGES, A "CULT OF THE BANNER" DEVELOPED IN KAZAKHSTAN. TODAY, SOME OF THE COUNTRY'S CURRENCY – THE 50-TENGE NOTE – CARRIES THAT IMAGE. THIS PETROGLYPH IS AT SHAKBAK-ATA IN THE MANGHYSTAU REGION.

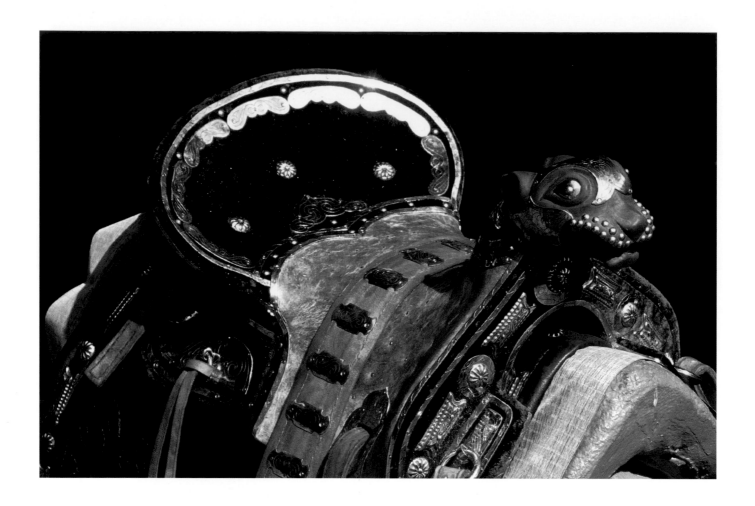

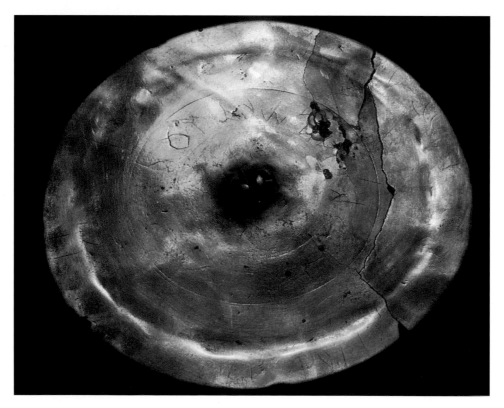

THIS SKIFF-STYLE SADDLE IS A REPRODUCTION OF ONE FOUND IN THE SEMIRECHYE AREA DATING FROM THE 9TH TO THE 10TH CENTURY A.D. AND FEATURING A SNOW LEOPARD HEAD. IT WAS MADE IN ALMATY BY THE KOULMANOV BROTHERS.

THIS BRONZE MIRROR WAS FOUND IN A WOMAN'S GRAVE OF THE KIPCHAK (TURKIC) TRIBE IN THE ZEVAKINSKY BURIAL MOUND IN EASTERN KAZAKHSTAN. IT DATES TO THE 9TH OR 10TH CENTURY A.D. ITS RUNIC INSCRIPTION READS, "THE NOBLE LADY LOSES HER FEELINGS OF ENVY; HER HAPPY TIMES ARE COMING." IT REFERS TO A SUPERSTITION THAT LOOKING IN A MIRROR TAKES AWAY EVIL FEELINGS. EAST KAZAKHSTAN REGIONAL HISTORICAL MUSEUM, ÖSKEMEN.

ANCIENT TRIBES USED ANIMALS AS SYMBOLS ON THEIR WEAPONS, CLOTHING AND TEXTILE PATTERNS. THE SAKA DAGGER ON THE LEFT, MADE OF METEORITE IRON, FEATURES GRIFFINS AND DATES TO THE 3RD CENTURY B.C. THE CENTER DAGGER FEATURES A HORSE, AND THE DAGGER AT RIGHT, A RAM. BOTH ARE BRONZE FROM THE SEMENSK-TURBINSK CULTURE IN THE 12TH TO 10TH CENTURIES B.C.

EAST KAZAKHSTAN REGIONAL HISTORICAL MUSEUM, OSKEMEN.

THE FRONT OF THE GOLDEN WARRIOR'S HEADDRESS COMBINES THE POWERFUL SYMBOLS OF A WINGED HORSE WITH THE HORNS
OF A MOUNTAIN GOAT. IT IS MADE OF WOOD AND GOLD SHEET AND IS CARVED, FORGED AND ENGRAVED.
IT MEASURES 10 X 17.5 CENTIMETERS (4 X 7 INCHES).

ANOTHER HEADDRESS DECORATION IS A STAMPED AND ENGRAVED GOLD PLAQUE THAT FEATURES MOUNTAINS AND A SNOW LEOPARD.

THE GOLDEN WARRIOR WORE A GOLD SEAL RING OF THE SUN GOD MITRA ON THE MIDDLE FINGER OF HIS RIGHT HAND. ON HIS
FOURTH FINGER HE WORE A GOLD MIRROR OR SOLAR RING. BOTH ARE CAST, ENGRAVED AND POLISHED. ALL THREE IMAGES ON THIS
PAGE ARE RARE PHOTOGRAPHS OF THE ORIGINAL ARTIFACTS. MUSEUM OF ARCHAEOLOGY, ALMATY.

"THE GOLDEN WARRIOR," A 5TH CENTURY B.C. SAKA CHIEFTAIN, WAS FOUND SPLENDIDLY PRESERVED IN 1969 IN THE ISSÏQ BURIAL MOUND NEAR ALMATY AT THE FOOT OF THE TIEN SHAN MOUNTAINS OVERLOOKING MOUNT TALGAR. HIS ELABORATELY DECORATED GOLD UNIFORM AND HEAD-DRESS CONTAIN A COMPLEX ARRAY OF SYMBOLS REPRESENTING MILITARY, POLITICAL AND SPIRITUAL IDEAS. DR. KEMAL A. AKISHEV LED THE EXCAVATION. REPRODUCTION BY KRYM ALTYNBEKOV.

MUSEUM OF ARCHEOLOGY, ALMATY.

THIS SAKA BURIAL MOUND AT SERGEYEVKA IN NORTHERN KAZAKHSTAN DATES TO THE 5TH CENTURY B.C. THIS SITE IS SIMILAR TO THE ISSÏQ BURIAL MOUND WHERE THE GOLDEN WARRIOR WAS DISCOVERED.

THIS SMALL, SACRED BRONZE-CAST LAMPION WAS USED TO BURN OIL AND INCENSE. A SQUATTING HORSEMAN WEARS A CAFTAN AND A HELMET-LIKE HAT. A MOVABLE HORSE FIGURE WITH A BRIDLE AND A PLAITED MANE HAS A HOLE IN ITS BACK FOR A CANDLE OR A TORCH. THE DISH IS 25.5 CENTIMETERS (10 INCHES) IN DIAMETER AND 18 CENTIMETERS (7 INCHES) HIGH. IT DATES FROM THE 4TH TO THE 3RD CENTURIES B.C. CENTRAL STATE MUSEUM, ALMATY.

THIS CAST COPPER CAULDRON WITH RAM'S HEAD LEGS DATES FROM THE 5TH TO THE 3RD CENTURIES B.C. IT WAS FOUND IN 1912 IN THE SEMIRECHYE AREA. IT STANDS 58.5 CENTIMETERS HIGH (23 INCHES). IT IS 31.5 CENTIMETERS (12 INCHES) DEEP AND 52 CENTIMETERS (20 INCHES) IN DIAMETER. CAULDRONS SUCH AS THIS WERE USED TO COOK THE MEAT OF SACRIFICIAL ANIMALS, OR AT THE START OF SEASONAL EVENTS SUCH AS THE SPRING FESTIVAL OF NAURÏZ. CENTRAL STATE MUSEUM, ALMATY.

THIS GOLD AND
TURQUOISE BACTRIAN
CAMEL RING DATES FROM
THE UYSUN TRIBAL PERIOD
IN THE 2ND CENTURY B.C.
IT WAS DISCOVERED AT
THE KARGALIN SITE.
CENTRAL STATE MUSEUM, ALMATY.

THIS HEADBAND OF GOLD FROM THE 2ND CENTURY B.C. IS INLAID WITH TURQUOISE, ALMANDINE AND CARVED WOOD. CALLED THE
KARGALIN DIADEM, IT WAS FOUND IN THE GRAVE OF A SHAMAN BELIEVED TO BE FEMALE. IT IS DECORATED WITH ANIMALS, AND THE
CENTRAL PORTION, WHICH HAS BEEN LOST, IS BELIEVED TO BE A TREE OF LIFE. IT WAS DISCOVERED IN THE MOUNTAINS AT KARGALIN AT
AN ALTITUDE OF 2,500 METERS (8,200 FEET). CENTRAL STATE MUSEUM, ALMATY.

SHAKBAK-ATA WAS ORIGI-
NALLY A ZOROASTRIAN
TEMPLE WHERE RITUALS
FOCUSED ON FIRE AS THE
SOURCE OF LIFE AND A
SYMBOL OF THE STRUGGLE
BETWEEN LIGHT AND DARK,
GOOD AND EVIL. DURING
THE 13TH CENTURY IT
EVOLVED INTO A MOSQUE
AND SUFI SCHOOL. TODAY
PILGRIMS COME HERE TO
SPEND THE NIGHT IN
MEDITATION AND PRAYER.
THE MAN-MADE HOLE IN
THE CENTER OF THE CEILING
IS SIMILAR IN PURPOSE TO
THE **SHANGÏRAQ** IN THE
YURT. IT IS CONSIDERED A
WINDOW TO ONE'S ANCES-
TORS AND THE GREAT
SPIRIT. THE TEMPLE IS NEAR
SHAKBAK CANYON IN THE
MANGHYSTAU REGION OF
WESTERN KAZAKHSTAN.

LARGE **BALBAL** SCULPTURES SERVED A VARIETY OF PURPOSES INCLUDING MEMORIALS AT GRAVE SITES, DEIFICATION OF ANCESTORS, MONUMENTS TO HONOR A DEFEATED ENEMY OR TRIBAL BOUNDARY MARKERS. TOP LEFT: A 6TH CENTURY B.C. **BALBAL** FOUND NEAR TARAZ DEPICTS THE GODDESS UMAY, PROTECTRESS OF MOTHERS AND FERTILITY. TOP RIGHT: A GRANITE **BALBAL** MARKING A GRAVE NEAR DIRIZHABL DATES FROM THE 8TH CENTURY B.C. BOTTOM RIGHT: AN 8TH-7TH CENTURY B.C. **BALBAL** FOUND IN SEMIRECHYE HOLDS A CUP SYMBOLIZING ABUNDANCE IN THE NEXT WORLD. BOTTOM LEFT: A 5TH-2ND B.C. **BALBAL** FOUND AT BAITE WELL, USTYURT PLATEAU, DEPICTS A FEMALE WARRIOR CHIEFTAIN.

THIS MARBLE MONUMENT IN ORDABASY IN SOUTHERN KAZAKHSTAN COMMEMORATES THE SITE WHERE ELDERS OF THE THREE KAZAKH HORDES, TOLE BI, KAZYBEK BI AND AYTEKE BI, UNITED IN 1726 TO FIGHT THE DZUNGARS (MONGOLS). THE LARGE PEDESTAL, 28 METERS (92 FEET) HIGH AND EIGHT METERS (26 FEET) SQUARE, SYMBOLIZES THE EARTH, WHICH GAVE BIRTH TO THESE THREE SONS OF THE KAZAKH PEOPLE.

ONE OF CENTRAL ASIA'S LARGEST DOMED MOSQUES HONORS HODJA AKHMED YASAVI, THE 12TH CENTURY SUFI MYSTIC WHOSE POETRY AND WRITINGS HAD TREMENDOUS IMPACT THROUGHOUT THAT PART OF THE WORLD. IT WAS COMMISSIONED IN 1390 BY TAMERLANE, THE TURKIC CONQUEROR, TO HONOR YASAVI AND SERVE AS HIS MAUSOLEUM. THE MOSQUE WAS BUILT IN EIGHT INDEPENDENT SECTIONS, WHICH HAS HELPED IT SURVIVE NUMEROUS EARTHQUAKES. THE BUILDING MEASURES 46.5 X 65.6 METERS (152 X 215 FEET). ITS WALLS ARE 2 METERS (6.5 FEET) THICK AND THE CENTRAL HALL WALLS ARE 3 METERS (10 FEET) THICK. THE DOME IS 37.5 METERS (123 FEET) HIGH AND 18.2 METERS (60 FEET) IN DIAMETER. THE DOME IS COVERED IN GLAZED, PATTERNED TURQUOISE TILES. IT IS LOCATED IN TURKESTAN IN SOUTHERN KAZAKHSTAN.

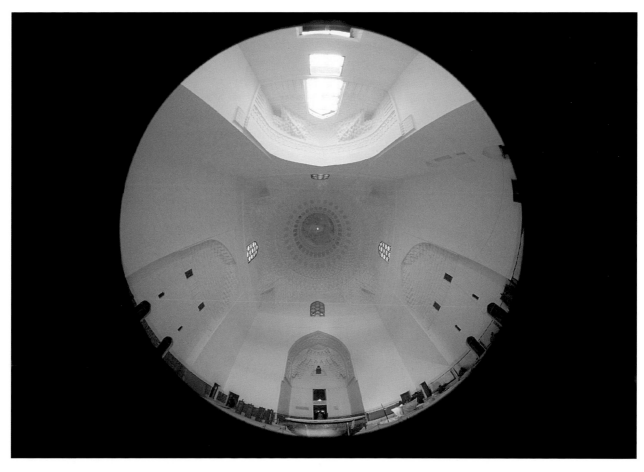

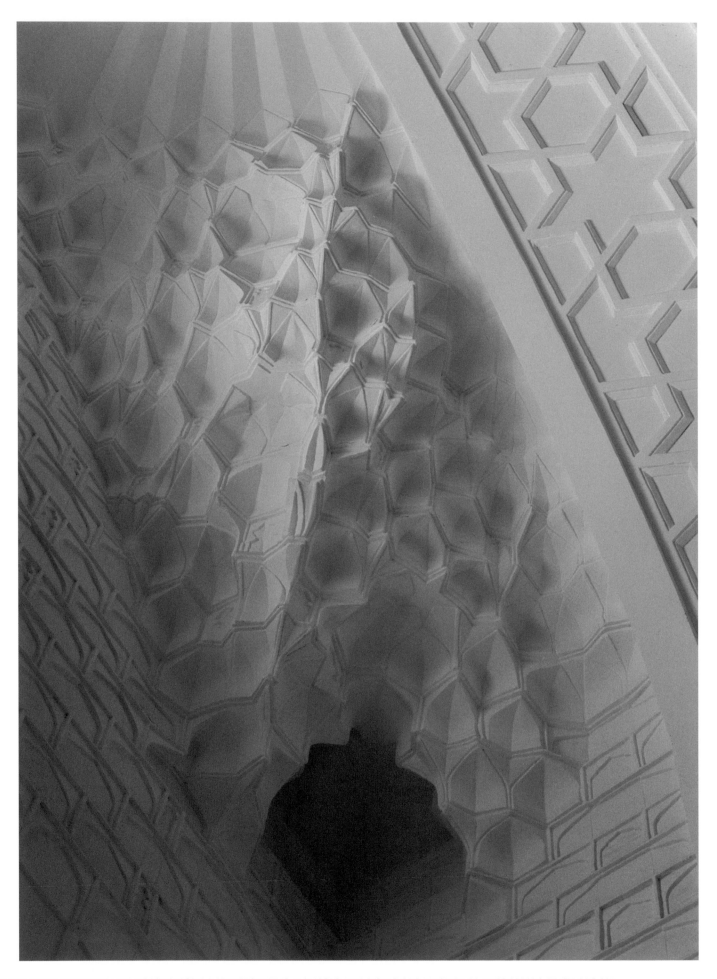

THESE ELEGANT NICHE-LIKE DECORATIONS JUST BELOW THE MAUSOLEUM'S DOME ARE KNOWN AS **MUQARNAS**. THEY ARE AN
ISLAMIC INVENTION THAT REACHED A ZENITH AROUND THE 13TH CENTURY. THE DELICATE AND SOARING DESIGNS EVOKE
YASAVI'S TRANSCENDENT AND COMPLEX POETRY AS WELL AS THE MYSTICAL IDEAS OF SUFISM.

PARTS OF THE MAUSOLEUM'S WALLS ARE ALSO COVERED WITH BLUE AND TURQUOISE MAJOLICA TILES LIKE THOSE USED ON THE DOME'S EXTERIOR. THEY ARE SIMILAR TO THE TILES USED ON THE DOMES OF THE FAMOUS MOSQUE AT SAMARKAND IN UZBEKISTAN. HERE, A GLAZED TAN, BROWN AND BLACK PATTERN OF BRICK ADORNS THE CEILINGS OF A SIDE-ENTRANCE GABLE.

KAZAKH MUSLIMS REGARD THE 11TH CENTURY MOSQUE NAMED AFTER ARYSTAN BAB AS THE HOLY OF HOLIES IN KAZAKHSTAN.
THIS MUSLIM CLERIC LIVED IN OTRAR IN SOUTHERN KAZAKHSTAN DURING THE 11TH CENTURY AND IS CREDITED WITH THE
PEACEFUL SPREAD OF ISLAM, AND THROUGH IT, OF THE ARABIC LANGUAGE AND ALPHABET. HE WAS THE TEACHER OF HODJA
AKHMED YASAVI. PILGRIMS TO TURKESTAN FIRST STOP AT THE ARYSTAN BAB MAUSOLEUM.

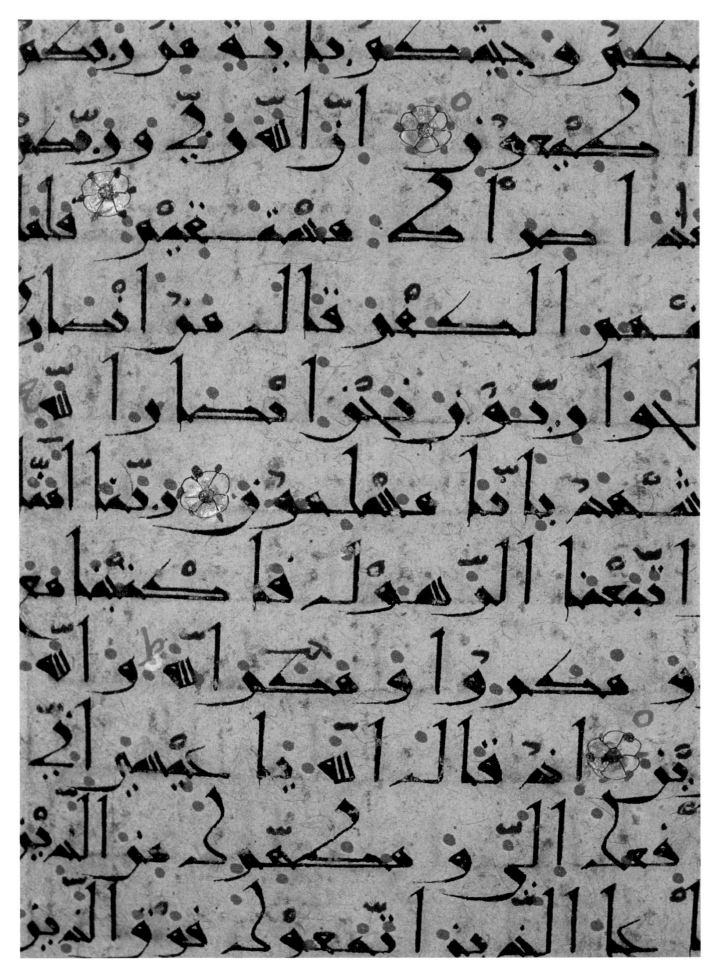

THIS KORAN IN THE ILLUMINATED STYLE WAS WRITTEN IN KUFIC IN THE 12TH CENTURY. IT MEASURES 32 X 39.5 CENTIMETERS (12.5 X 15.5 INCHES). IT WAS ORIGINALLY AT THE HODJA AKHMED YASAVI MOSQUE IN TURKESTAN.

RARE BOOK SECTION, NATIONAL LIBRARY OF KAZAKHSTAN, ALMATY.

## TRADITIONAL LIFE: A DAILY CELEBRATION OF HERITAGE

Until the beginning of the 20th century the traditional life of most Kazakhs was spent in the universal dwelling of the nomads – the yurt.

The yurt is one of the most unique achievements of human genius. Only one who has experienced the yurt *in life* – in its various seasons and states and meanings – can appreciate the emotional ties to this traditional dwelling. Try to picture yourself in the following scenarios:

*After a long journey in deep snow, in the windy chill of a gray winter evening, you arrive home and step into the warmth of the bright, spacious, radiantly colored yurt; the aroma of fresh bread and a pot of et (meat stew) simmering on the fire tantalizes the hollow in your stomach....*

*After enduring the feverish intensity of summer heat at noon when everything is silent and it seems that even time is standing still, you step into the dry, cool semidarkness of a yurt; you fall onto the cool surface of silken comforters and dip into an aromatic bowl of astringent, frothy cold kumiss (qïmïz)....*

*You awaken early on a spring morning with the joyous sensation of sunlight streaming on your face through the sky opening of the yurt; you arise and emerge from the door, shivering in the chill of the morning, trembling with the expectation that life awaits you, and greet the rising sun over a vast, blossoming steppe....*

Only a person who has experienced these events and felt their impact can completely appreciate how the yurt animates Kazakh life. The yurt is a model and a symbol of humanity and the universe, and it contains within it most of the clues to nomadic civilization. Although its structure appears to be quite simple, given these declarations, it is worthy of a detailed look.

SILK AND VELVET YURT ROOF STRAPS

The word *yurt* as the name of a dwelling entered world usage through the Russian language. In Kazakh, the word *zhurt* literally means "community, family, relatives or people." The actual physical dwelling is referred to as *kiyiz üy*, which means "felt home"; or *qara üy*, meaning "large home"; or *qazaqï üy*, which means "Kazakh home."

Nomadic life would be impossible without a dwelling that was transportable in one way or another, of course. One of the early models is described by Herodotus, the father of history, in his account of the campaign of the Scythians against the Persian armies of Darius in the 5th century B.C. He mentions felt dwellings on carts, which were one of the types of dwellings known historically in Western Eurasia, including parts of what is today Kazakhstan. His description is echoed in the "felt Turkic carts" described by Friar William of Rubruck, envoy of France's King Louis IX from 1252 to 1254, who traveled the Kazakh steppes on a journey to Karakorum, the Mongolian capital of Chingis Khan.

The width of the base of a cart capable of carrying a felt home was 9 meters (30 feet), and it was pulled by 33 pairs of oxen. Such constructions were probably very comfortable, but not very convenient given how cumbersome they were and the slow pace at which they would have had to travel. Smaller versions of this type of dwelling survived among the Nogai until the beginning of the 20th century.

Some scholars believe that a genuine revolution occurred in the middle of the first millennium A.D. with the development of the collapsible yurt. This is basically the ingenious structure that is still in use in variations today. The wooden framework of this type of yurt consists of a *kerege*, or folding lattice around the circumference that supports the walls; roof poles that extend from the ground to the smokehole called an *uwïq*; and a round frame that holds the structure together at the top known as a *shangïraq* or roof-hole frame, which serves simultaneously as a hole for venting smoke and a "sky window" for the structure. Together with the framed opening for the door called an *esik* and the six *baqan*, or pole staffs used to raise the *shangïraq*, all of these items form the yurt's skeleton. This frame is built from a variety of woods such as willow, birch, bird cherry and poplar. Covered with white felt richly ornamented in brightly colored designs and situated on the emerald-green grass of a mountain slope, the Kazakh yurt frequently resembles a bird alighted upon a slope to rest.

In Kazakhstan there are two kinds of yurts: the Kazakh and the Kalmyk. The latter is distinguished by its conical roof, similar to the American Indian teepee, which is created by the straight poles used to support the *shangïraq*; in form, this is closer to the Mongol type of yurt. The Turkic and the later Kazakh yurt has a hemispherical roof.

SILK AND VELVET YURT ROOF STRAP

Assembling a yurt is a magic act of the First Creation – the transformation of Chaos into the Cosmos, Disorder into Order. Each step in the process has symbolic meaning and the participants are keenly aware of this.

Two or three women set up the yurt over a period of several hours. First they set up the wooden door frame, to which they attach the lattice framework known as the *qanat*, or wing. The size of the yurt depends upon the number of sections of lattice framework that are used. An average yurt consists of six *qanat* and can easily accommodate up to 20 people. The exquisitely ornamented yurts of the khans could consist of as

many as 12 to 14 lattice wings and were intended for large gatherings.

The second step is the raising of the *shangïraq*, or roof-hole frame, which is similar in function to the keystone of an arch. For this, the *baqan*, the six curved poles with a fork at the end, are used. The raising of the *shangïraq* is the duty of the head of the household or of the elder of the clan. Typically birch is chosen to build the *shangïraq*, cut no later than the middle of summer when the wood is filled with sap and can be bent. All the other elements of the yurt are replaced when they become unfit for use; but the *shangïraq* always remains the same, becoming a sort of family heirloom passed down from generation to generation as it grows darker in color from the smoke of the hearth fire.

The *shangïraq* and each of its details have their own symbolic significance. For example, its crossed framework – the sturdy support planks placed at right angles to one another around the circumference of the *shangïraq* – creates four points, each directed toward a corner of the world. The entire circular roof-hole frame serves not only as a smokehole and window, but also as a kind of "steppe observatory" since nomads view stars through it to determine when to move from one pasturage to another.

The third step in setting up the yurt is to secure the lattice framework of the walls and the roof-hole frame to the curved wooden poles. The upper, narrow tips of the poles fit into slots in the roof-hole frame, while the lower ones fasten to the lattice

framework.

In order to test the sturdiness of the set-up, a swing is attached to the rim of the roof-hole frame, and a 6- or 7-year-old-boy and girl swing on it together while the women gather around and try to make them laugh. The swinging and the laughter of the children are intended to bring blessings of fertility and happiness to the newly established home.

The walls of the yurt are covered all around with decorated reed mats that give protection from the wind, and a second felt door (*kiyiz esik*) is hung on the interior of the doorway. The wooden and felt parts of the yurt are held together with decorative woven ribbons made of textile or carpets that give the yurt truly the appearance of a "felt home."

The hemispherical roof of the yurt is a symbol of the firmament with the sun in its center, while the *shangïraq* is the equivalent of the family. Normally the *shangïraq* is inherited by the *kenzhe*, or youngest son, and his home is considered foremost since it will pass the family *shangïraq* along to future generations. Thus the youngest son is also known as *shangïraq üyesi*, or lord of the *shangïraq*. Tradition dictates that guests visit his yurt, which retains the primary family *shangïraq*, before they visit the homes of his older brothers; it is a sign of respect as well since the elderly parents also live with the youngest son. Frequently three generations of one family lived together – the elders, the younger generation and their children.

The yurt is also anthropomorphized. Its parts are called by the names of parts of the human body. Thus the center of the yurt, the place of the hearth, is known as the *kindik*, or navel; the walls of the yurt are called *bökse*, or thighs; the interior of the lattice frame is known as the "womb," or *qarïn*; the roof is called *ïyïq*, or shoulders; the opening in the *shangïraq* is called *köz*, or eye; the wooden frame is known either as *süyek*, meaning bones, or *qanqa*, which means skeleton; and the felt covering is called *zhabu*, or clothing. Each yurt is said to have its own spirit; and thus when guests enter they must bow their heads and pronounce greetings, even if nobody is home.

The area within the yurt has a sacred character and is imbued with its own symbolism, too. The spot opposite the entrance is the *tör*, or place of honor. As the Kazakhs say, *"Törge shïghïngïz,"* or "Go up to the *tör*" – in other words, "Please take the place of honor." This is where people who are closer to the Upper World by virtue of their social status, age or artistic gifts are seated. This place allows the honored one to survey the entire area, with men seated along the right side of the yurt and women along the left. The spot closest to the door is where people who are nearest socially to the Lower World (poor people, sick people and others) are seated. Once again, the Upper, Middle and Lower Worlds of cosmology reveal their universality in Kazakh philosophy and tradition.

At the center, or navel, of the yurt is the hearth, which should never be crossed, even when it is not lit. The hearth is a sacred area, the place of fire over which the worldly axis passes and unites the Upper, Middle, and Lower Worlds. It is along this axis that the lives of the inhabitants of the felt dwelling, and of life itself, rotate.

To the left of the entrance to the yurt – on the right from the interior perspective facing the door – women give birth to children, supported by a horse harness stretched between the lattice frame of the wall and the *baqan* poles. Even newborn livestock are brought here to warm up. Children of both sexes are generally with their mothers on the female side of the yurt until ages 6 or 7. From ages 7 to 12 there is no fixed place for them to be – it is arbitrary; after that, the sons, as full-fledged members of male society, switch to the men's side where the father is.

On the right side of the yurt is the riding harness and saddle of the head of the household; in the house of a hunter, his equipment would be kept here, too, including his hunting bird or dog. In the central portion of the right side of the yurt is the bed of the young family, closed off with a *shïmïldïq*, or embroidered curtain. The right side is also the place for young married people, including daughters of the head of the household of marriageable age.

It should be noted here that women held a high social status in nomadic society. The woman was not just the keeper of the hearth, but its mistress. Kazakh women never wore a veil (such as the Uzbek *paranja*) or similar garment. Instead, they participated equally with men in performing the exhausting daily chores, were responsible for disassembling and reassembling the yurt, prepared stores of food for the whole year, ran the household, and – most important of all – they were mothers. A mother was illuminated by a halo of sanctity and grandeur that accorded her a relationship of respect from childhood until old age. Young girls were cherished and treated with attentiveness since they were simply considered guests in their own home, having been born for their future husband's family. Thus the parents' mission was to teach her how to build her future happiness. By a young age, girls were already skilled at traditional crafts and riding horses.

The *tör*, or place of honor in the yurt, is in the middle of the area opposite to and farthest from the door. It is put together with trunks covered with rolled-up carpets and comforters. This spot in the yurt provides the best protection against attack from without as well as from within. According to Kazakh rules of hospitality, the guest is under the full protection of the host, who is expected to protect the guest even at the cost of his own life if necessary.

To the left of the place of honor is the bed for the elders, and closer to the entrance is the place for dishes and food stores. Every item in a yurt has its own special area, just as each individual knows his or her own place in the social and age hierarchy of the community and occupies his or her own special position and function within the life of the social group.

Today the yurt remains indispensable as a summer dwelling in agricultural areas of Kazakhstan and as the basic dwelling of the few remaining nomadic or herding groups. But in urban life, interestingly, many of the symbolic signs of the ancient nomadic dwelling are preserved. Thus in many modern homes and apartments, in the room used for entertaining guests, a table is placed in the middle of this space farthest from the entrance. The head place at that table is still referred to – just as centuries ago – as the *tör*, or place of honor, and it is richly decorated and reserved for honored guests. The order for seating guests also often follows the old system: Guests take their places according to regulated tradition – high to low status and male to female – and the behavior of guests is regulated by ancient rituals as well. Some of the urban population are already losing these traditions; and furniture and many other items in the urban apartment have changed in modern times, as well, of course.

In the traditional yurt, every single item had not only symbolic importance, but a strong functional value for the nomad as well. Thus the world of people and the world of objects were bound inseparably in the yurt and by the yurt. The yurt was not just a place of "residence," but a home full of life – a place of daily work and rest, of festivities and holidays, of socializing and the taking of meals.

Food consumed by the yurt dwellers was a high-protein diet consisting predominantly of meat and milk products. Such food

provided the energy people needed to engage in hard physical labor. Kazakhs consume the meat of sheep, horses and camels, and the means for preserving these items were developed over many centuries. The nomads begin to lay meat in store – the *soghïm*, or slaughter of animals for winter – with the beginning of cold weather in November and December. For better preservation and for religious reasons the meat is drained of blood and dried as much as possible. The meat is cut into chunks, salted and dried; and only then is it put into cold storage covered with wormwood, or cured with juniper smoke. Horse sausage called *qazï* (traditionally consisting of an entire rib with meat, encased in intestine), *shuzhïq* (pieces of meat with fat and spices), and *zhaya* (meat from the neck of the horse) are considered delicacies. *Quwïrdaq* is made from the heart, liver, kidneys, tripe and other leftover cuts of meat fried in fresh sheep fat.

Kazakhs often eat boiled meat. The most basic dish is called *et*, or meat. The recipe for this dish is surprisingly simple: Large pieces of meat on the bone are slowly simmered in salted water at a gentle boil; then layers of thin rolled dough (*qamïr*) are put into this soup to cook; and at the presentation everything is smothered with an oniony broth. And is that it? Yes, but the secret is to be found in the quality, amount and combination of meat for *besbarmaq* – literally "five fingers," as the Russians came to call this dish, because the Kazakhs ate it with their hands.

Just as an experienced Kazakh

will find beauty and nuances in the open steppe or the endless desert that the inhabitants of a noisy, crowded city might find monotonous, an experienced Kazakh will find in *et* an endless variety of tastes, aromas and nuances. Sophisticated palates can often discern the slightest variations in the taste of the dish as a result of the age of the livestock, the pastures on which the herd grazed, the method used to preserve the meat, and the art of preparing the dish. Simply stated, even by the taste of the *sorpa*, or broth – which is served separately as a bowl of bouillon – connoisseurs can also discern a lot about their host.

KUMISS LADLE

A similar phenomenal variety can be found in the dairy foods of the Kazakhs. First of all is the legendary kumiss (*qïmïz*), which nomads have fondly venerated since the time of the Scythians. This fermented mare's milk – astringent, frothy, with a slight sour taste – often reminds Europeans or Americans of beer. Kumiss has practically the same range of variety as beer as a result of the various characteristics of the milk and the method and period of fermentation. The longer it is kept, the higher the percentage of alcohol.

The primary difference between kumiss and beer is in the medicinal properties of kumiss. As Kazakhs like to joke, the only thing kumiss cannot cure is death. One of the best-known medicinal qualities of kumiss is its clear antitubercular properties. Currently in Eurasia, there are two official centers for kumiss therapy: One is in the Kökshetau district of Kazakhstan in Burabay, and the other is in Bashqortostan in the Russian Federation where tuberculosis is successfully treated with a four-month course of kumiss therapy. Another secret about kumiss is its aphrodisiac properties: Kumiss has long had a reputation among Kazakhs as a natural means for combating aging and impotence.

Fermented camel's milk, known as *shubat*, has a soft, velvety taste and a slightly thick texture that can never be forgotten once you've tried it. It is the best means to regain strength after an illness. It is also used to treat diabetes and illnesses of the immune system.

Kazakhs consume all four kinds of milk – from sheep, cows, camels and mares – separately and in combination, but in its fresh form it is generally used as a creamer for tea. The number of different kinds of milk products in the Kazakh diet is truly without end. This includes *qaymaq* (skimmed or boiled cream), *ayran* and *qatïq* (milk products soured using a culture like kefir or yogurt), and *süzbe* and *irimshik* (which are like cottage cheese). The latter, when salted and carefully strained through cheese-cloth, formed into round balls or loaves and dried in the sun, is called *qurt* and can be preserved for years. Kazakh children also like *qurt*, just as modern urban children love chewing gum. Once softened and mixed with bouillon or hot water, *qurt* also can serve as a separate dish all by itself. In addition, it has an indispensable curative property against colds; it works against cough and fever by encouraging the body to sweat profusely and, as a result, get well.

Butter that has been made in wooden churns is filtered, washed in water, salted, and preserved in dry sheep or horse intestines. Such butter, kept for a long time, absorbs enzymes from the intestinal fibers. It does not get rancid because the intestines can "breathe." Over time it also became a medicinal ointment that could be applied to surface wounds and even to the most serious open wounds.

MAKING FRIED BREAD

Bread baked on coals or a *tandïr* (a round clay oven) or fried in fat is the symbol of the home, of protection and wealth. If there is bread on the *dastarqan* – the ceremonial tablecloth laid on the ground – the most essential food has already been served. It should be eaten immediately as a way to show respect for the bread. When establishing new kinship relations with a daughter-in-law or when adopting a child, the mother embraces the person while holding hot fried bread to her bosom; when sending a husband off to war or a son to the army, women send along with them a specially baked ritual bread to ensure their loved one's safe return. Kazakhs swear by bread, tell fortunes by bread, and curse by bread. The aroma of the hot fat in which *shelpek* (flat bread) is fried – which tradition says should be prepared only in batches of the magical number seven (7, 14, 21, etc.) – is a special occasion in itself because its aroma is the food of the *aruaq*, the spirits of the ancestors. And the round balls of leavened dough fried in fat, the golden *bauïrsaqs* scattered across the *dastarqan*, are the pride and joy of each hostess.

The traditional food of the Kazakhs is not only the means of physical survival, but symbolic of spiritual nourishment as well. It is a symphony of tastes, customs and rituals absorbed through each meal since childhood that has served as the cornerstone and foundation of the Kazakh consciousness.

The culmination of Kazakh traditional culture is in the country's renowned hospitality rituals, and at the center of those is the shared meal. This is a special time in which an organized social group, in an organized universe, carefully assembles around a *dastarqan*. The ritual of seating guests in prescribed places around the yurt gives a full picture of the social and family relations of the individuals there, and as mentioned earlier, demonstrates the group's hierarchy and priorities.

The boiled head of a sheep is served to the most honored guest or elder, who divides it into pieces and distributes it with blessings to all the participants. Each guest receives a part of the sheep in accordance with his or her social status and age. For example, the son-in-law, or *küyeu*, is always given the tender rib meat; the young daughter-in-law, or *kelin*, gets the *quyïmshaq*, or last vertebra; and the children are given the ears, so that they will listen, and the tongue, so that they will be eloquent; and so on.

Kazakh hospitality rituals are strictly observed; they are the fundamental occasion for social communication in traditional society. It is during this time that Kazakhs exchange news: Guests are required to talk about themselves and their travels, and about events where they live. The genealogical ties between the hosts and the guests are discussed thoroughly, and historical legends and stories are told. In the steppes there is the unique form of transmitting information known as the *uzïn qulaq,* or "long ear" – whatever is discussed seated around the *dastarqan* will be known the next day for hundreds of miles around! How? By what

means? Who knows?!

Sharing food around the *dastarqan* is not only a time for conversation, it is also a time for music making. An occasion for great rejoicing in any household is a visit by a *zhïrau*, or teller of epic tales, or a musician known as a *küyshi*, either of whom become

SHAMAN WITH QOBÏZ

the center of the occasion. Even in modern cities it is difficult to imagine gathering around a Kazakh table without long monologues by guests on philosophical topics, usually in the form of detailed toasts and good wishes, as well as the singing of beloved traditional songs.

Modern urban life has inevitably introduced changes into the traditional Kazakh menu. Together with the common Central Asian *plov* (rice pilaf with onions, carrots and meat) and *mantï* (steamed meat or vegetable dumplings), the Kazakh diet now includes cold appetizers

such as baked chicken, meat or fish in aspic, an abundance of salads, marinated vegetables, a variety of homemade or store-bought baked goods, jams and candies, and soft drinks such as Coca-Cola, Sprite and Fanta, as well as locally produced drinks. Almaty and other large cities are quite cosmopolitan. Despite this, as before, no Kazakh gathering is complete without traditional sweets prepared according to old recipes and saved especially for guests.

Just as an ocean can be recognized in each drop of saltwater, so is the soul of Kazakhstan manifested in each element of its culture. The mark and essence of Kazakh ethnicity is the living space that is defined by the laws of the Kazakh yurt, the native cuisine at the traditional gathering around the table, the poetry of good wishes and the voice of the mother singing a lullaby – all are filled with meaning and symbolism in the Kazakh view of the universe and life. It is reflected in their history and embodied in their present.

THE **SHANGÏRAQ** IS THE FUNCTIONAL KEYSTONE THAT HOLDS THE YURT TOGETHER. BUT IT ALSO SYMBOLIZES THE HEARTH OF THE HOME AND THE WHEEL OF THE SUN. THE OPENING PROVIDES AN OBSERVATORY THROUGH WHICH TO READ THE STARS AND TELL TIME; AND SPIRITUALLY, IT DIRECTS ONE'S ATTENTION TO THE SKY AND TENGRI, THE SKY GOD.

THE FIRST STEP IN ASSEMBLING A YURT IS TO ATTACH THE LATTICE WALL SECTIONS TO THE DOOR FRAME AS VILLAGERS ARE DOING HERE IN SHIELI IN THE QÏZÏLORDA REGION. THE DOOR OF A YURT ALWAYS LOOKS TO THE EAST SO THAT THE SUN IS THE FIRST VISITOR TO THE NOMAD'S HOME.

WOMEN MAKE MANY OF THE YURT'S PARTS BY HAND: STRAPS, FELT COVER, TEXTILES, **CHI** AND RUGS. THEY ALSO TAKE THE LEAD IN ITS ASSEMBLY AS SEEN HERE IN SHIELI. SIX PEOPLE CAN ASSEMBLE A YURT IN ABOUT THREE HOURS.

THE VARIOUS MATERIALS AND LAYERS THAT COVER THE YURT SERVE FUNCTIONS SIMILAR TO DRESSING IN LAYERS OF CLOTHING FOR THE WEATHER. THE REED MATS SERVE AS A FILTER, THE FELT IS INSULATION AND THE COTTON OR SILK COVER REFLECTS THE SUN AND ULTRAVIOLET RAYS.

THE YURT IS A UNIQUE STRUCTURE, A PHYSICAL AND METAPHORICAL EXPRESSION OF KAZAKH NOMADIC LIFE. IT IS AN OASIS OF LIFE AND COLOR, A NURTURING PLACE OF SAFETY WHERE FAMILY AND FRIENDS COME TOGETHER. IT IS IRONIC THAT THE YURT – A SMALL, SELF-CONTAINED STRUCTURE IN THE VASTNESS OF THE STEPPES – HAS WITHIN IT A GENEROUS SPACIOUSNESS. THE YURT IS WHERE ART, LIFE AND NATURE MERGE. THE ART STYLE IS MARKED BY ORNAMENTAL IMPROVISATION AND REFLECTS THE PASSIONATE, OPEN AND JOYFUL KAZAKH PERSONALITY. THE USE OF NATURAL MATERIALS ORDERED BY THE HUMAN HAND CREATES A HARMONY OF COLORS AND SHAPES MUCH LIKE A FLOWER ARRANGEMENT. TO LIVE INSIDE A YURT IS TO LIVE INSIDE ART.
CENTRAL STATE MUSEUM, ALMATY.

THIS SCHEMATIC PRESENTATION OF A YURT SHOWS HOW ITS PARTS WORK TOGETHER. LATTICE WALLS UNFOLD AND ARE STRAPPED TOGETHER. RIBS OF THE ROOF FIT INTO HOLES IN THE **SHANGÏRAQ** CIRCLE OVERHEAD AND ARE THEN LASHED TO THE CROSSPIECES OF THE WALL. THIS WOODEN FRAME IS THE SKELETON ON WHICH OUTER AND INNER COVERINGS AND OTHER ITEMS ARE HUNG. OUTSIDE IS A LAYER OF **CHI**, OR REED MATS, THEN A LAYER OF DECORATIVE FELT AND SOMETIMES A FINAL LAYER OF COTTON OR SILK. INSIDE, TEXTILES WITH ORNAMENTAL SCHEMES AND HOUSEHOLD ITEMS ARE HUNG ON THE LATTICEWORK. MANY FACTORS MAKE ONE FEEL COMFORTABLE AND SECURE INSIDE, PARTLY BECAUSE EACH PIECE IS NATURAL, HANDMADE, AND NO TOOLS ARE NEEDED FOR ITS ASSEMBLY.
KASTEYEV MUSEUM OF FINE ARTS, ALMATY.

TO BE KAZAKH IS TO
DECORATE. THE INTERIOR
OF A YURT IS A DESIGNER'S
PARADISE, AS CAN READILY
BE SEEN. THIS EXHIBIT IN
THE AKTAU MUSEUM MAY
BE THE APOTHEOSIS, BUT
IT IS A TRUE REFLECTION
OF THE SPECTACULAR
ORNAMENTATION THAT
THE KAZAKHS SEEM TO
INHERENTLY USE SO WELL.
REGIONAL HISTORY AND LOCAL
STUDIES MUSEUM, AKTAU,
MANGHYSTAU REGION.

A ONE-HOUR MIDAFTERNOON NAP BREAKS THE LONG SCHOOL DAY
OF ELEMENTARY STUDENTS AT THE ARKHIMED SCHOOL IN ALMATY.
THEY STUDY A WIDE CURRICULUM FROM 8 IN THE MORNING
UNTIL 6 IN THE EVENING.

THESE MISCHIEVOUS-LOOKING BOYS LIVE IN THE VILLAGE OF
AKMARAL IN KATON-KARAGAI IN NORTHEASTERN KAZAKHSTAN
WHERE RED DEER KNOWN AS **MARAL** ARE RAISED. THE VELVET
HARVESTED FROM THE ANTLERS OF THESE ANIMALS IS AN
EXPENSIVE INGREDIENT IN SOME ORIENTAL MEDICINES.

MANAP MYKHANOVA'S FACE SUGGESTS A LIFE OF HARD WORK THAT HAS BEEN MET WITH HUMOR AND GRACE. SHE LIVES IN THE VILLAGE OF SHIELI IN THE QÏZÏLORDA REGION AND IS ONE OF THOSE MATERNAL LEADERS WHO STRENGTHEN A COMMUNITY.

A WIDE VARIETY OF FACES MAKES A MOSAIC-LIKE PORTRAIT OF THE KAZAKH PEOPLE. TOP LEFT: A JUBILANT VILLAGER, MRS. AKHATOVA, IN BORLI-AUL; TOP RIGHT, A KAZAKH LANGUAGE STUDENT, ARKHIMED HIGH SCHOOL, ALMATY; BOTTOM LEFT, SHADAN TONBETOVA, A GRANDMOTHER IN SHIELI VILLAGE; AND BOTTOM RIGHT, SAULE ISKAKOVA, A HISTORY TEACHER IN KEGEN. "WHEN I SAW SAULE IN THE TOWN SQUARE, I WALKED OVER AND SAID, 'YOU HAVE A LOVELY FACE. MAY I TAKE YOUR PICTURE?' SHE ANSWERED, 'YES, BUT ONE MOMENT.' SHE RETRIEVED HER PASSPORT CONTAINING HER PHOTOGRAPH AS A YOUNG WOMAN. 'SEE,' SHE SAID, 'I USED TO BE PRETTY.' I RESPONDED, 'YOU'RE RIGHT, AND NOW YOU ARE BEAUTIFUL.' " – W.E.

KAZAKH FACES ALSO REFLECT THE MULTIETHNIC MELTING POT THE COUNTRY HAS BECOME OVER THE LAST CENTURY. TOP LEFT, DANA MAKHATOVA DOES GRADUATE RESEARCH AT THE NATIONAL LIBRARY; TOP RIGHT, ABDULKHAK TURLYBAYEV, WEARING A TRADITIONAL WINTER HAT CALLED A TÏMAQ, TRAINS EAGLES AS A PROFESSION AT HIS HOME NEAR ALMATY; BOTTOM LEFT, PERNEGUL OMAROVA, A HIGHLY REGARDED SCULPTOR, TURNED HER ART TO CREATING EXQUISITE DOLLS OF HISTORICAL KAZAKH FIGURES; BOTTOM RIGHT, ANOTHER KAZAKH LANGUAGE STUDENT AT ARKHIMED HIGH SCHOOL.

OWLS ARE REGARDED AS SACRED BIRDS IN PART BECAUSE OF THEIR VISION AND STEALTH. THEIR FEATHERS ARE USED ON CEREMONIAL HATS, MUSICAL INSTRUMENTS CALLED **DOMBÏRA** AND OTHER SPECIAL OBJECTS TO IMPART THE SPIRIT OF THE SACRED. THIS GREAT HORNED OWL IS ONE OF THE BIRDS OF PREY BELONGING TO ABDULKHAK TURLYBAYEV, THE "EAGLE MAN."

"THIS KAZAKH WORLD WAR II VETERAN BEDECKED WITH MEDALS WAS AT THE ÄUEZOV JUBILEE FESTIVAL. I SAW HIM AS I WAS LEAVING THE CELEBRATIONS AND ASKED HIM WHAT HE HAD GOTTEN ALL THE RIBBONS FOR. WITHOUT HESITATION HE ANSWERED, 'I FOUGHT THE NAZIS IN THE GREAT PATRIOTIC WAR AND WE DEFEATED THEM.' I PUT MY HAND OUT AND SAID, 'I WOULD LIKE TO THANK YOU FOR HELPING TO GIVE ME MY FREEDOM, TOO.' HE STRETCHED OUT HIS ARMS AND GAVE ME A WARM BEAR HUG. WHEN HE MOVED BACK, HIS EYES WERE FILLED WITH TEARS AND HE SAID, 'THANK YOU.' " – W.E.

KAZAKH CADETS FROM
BAURJAN MOMYSH-ULY
MILITARY SCHOOL ATTEND
A MEMORIAL CEREMONY AT
PANFILOV HEROES PARK IN
CENTRAL ALMATY. THE GLORY
MEMORIAL WITH ITS ETERNAL
FLAME COMMEMORATES,
AMONG OTHER HEROES, 28
KAZAKH SOLDIERS WHO
REPULSED 50 NAZI TANKS
ON THE OUTSKIRTS OF
MOSCOW IN 1941 DURING
THE GREAT PATRIOTIC WAR,
AS WORLD WAR II IS
KNOWN.

THESE FEMALE BACTRIAN CAMELS CAN WEIGH 450 TO 650 KILOGRAMS (1,000 TO 1,450 LB) AND STAND 190 TO 230 CENTIMETERS (75 TO 91 INCHES) TALL AT THE HUMP.

"THIS MALE BACTRIAN CAMEL POSTURED A WARNING TO ME TO KEEP MY DISTANCE FROM THE FEMALES IN HIS HAREM. THIS SPECIES ORIGINATED IN SOUTHERN KAZAKHSTAN AND WESTERN TURKESTAN AND WAS DOMESTICATED AROUND 2,500 B.C. THEIR UNIQUE CHARACTERISTICS HELP NOMADS SURVIVE IN THE DESERT. ON THIS PARTICULAR DAY IT WAS 26 DEGREES BELOW ZERO FAHRENHEIT IN THE STEPPES NORTH OF BAKANAS IN SOUTHEASTERN KAZAKHSTAN." – W.E.

A **SHABAN**, OR SHEPHERD, GUIDES HIS FLOCK THROUGH A MOUNTAIN PASS IN BUTAKOVKA IN THE ZAILIISKY ALATAU MOUNTAINS IN SOUTHEASTERN KAZAKHSTAN.

ZHYMABAI MUKHANOV DEMONSTRATES TRADITIONAL SHEEP SHEARING TO NURSULTAN ZHUMABAEV AND
FARIDA SAMETOVA IN THE VILLAGE OF SHIELI IN QÏZÏLORDA. THE SHEARS, CALLED **KYRYKTYK**,
ARE THE SAME AS THOSE USED IN OTHER NOMADIC CULTURES.

AN ELDERLY VENDOR CARRIES HER PAIL FULL OF **APORT** APPLES THROUGH A BIRCH GROVE TO SELL BY A ROADSIDE. **APORTS** COME FROM ORCHARDS OUTSIDE ALMATY WHERE TREES THAT CARRY THE GENES OF THE FIRST APPLES ARE STILL CULTIVATED.

AT 6:00 A.M. IN THE VILLAGE OF SHIELI, TEA IS PREPARED IN SAMOVARS WHILE ROUND BALLS OF LEAVENED DOUGH CALLED **BAUÏRSAQS** ARE DEEP-FRIED A GOLDEN BROWN.

A BASKET OF FRAGRANT **APORT** APPLES SITS IN THE SUN AT GORNYI SADOVOD FARM NEAR ALMATY.

THE **DASTARQAN** IS A BEAUTIFUL SPREAD OF FOOD PREPARED AND LAID ON A SPECIAL TABLECLOTH TO WELCOME GUESTS
INTO THE HOME, SUCH AS THIS ONE IN THE VILLAGE OF SHIELI IN QÏZÏLORDA.

A HONEY VENDOR AT THE ZELYONY BAZAAR (THE GREEN MARKET) IN ALMATY DOES HER BOOKKEEPING. KAZAKHSTAN
HAS AN ASTOUNDING VARIETY OF HONEY. A PROFUSION OF WILDFLOWERS AND BLOSSOMS PRODUCES
SOME OF THE MOST FLAVORFUL HONEY IN CENTRAL ASIA AND RUSSIA.

MODERN METHODS DOMINATE AGRICULTURE, BUT BEAUTIFUL RURAL SCENES LIKE THIS FAMILY GATHERING HAY NEAR PETROPAVL CAN STILL BE SEEN.

VENDORS OF NUTS, APRICOTS, RAISINS AND OTHER DRIED FRUITS GATHER IN ONE AREA OF THE ZELYONY BAZAAR IN ALMATY. THIS MARKET, ON THE ROUTE OF THE OLD SILK ROAD, IS AWASH WITH COLORS, AROMAS AND SOUNDS. SEPARATE AREAS HOUSE VENDORS SELLING VEGETABLES, HONEY, FRUIT, FLOWERS, MEAT AND FISH, HERBS AND SPICES AND DAIRY PRODUCTS.

WELCOMING GUESTS INTO ONE'S HOME, BE IT AN URBAN APARTMENT OR A YURT IN THE STEPPES, IS CONSIDERED AN HONOR. KAZAKH HOSPITALITY HAS EVOLVED INTO A REFINED ART. THIS BEAUTIFUL **DASTARQAN** IS IN THE HOME OF AMANGUL IKHANOVA AND ZHANGIR UMBETOV, ARTISANS IN ALMATY.

THIS RARE BALABAN FALCON CAME TO THE ATTENTION OF A WEALTHY ARAB FALCONER WHO OFFERED MR. TURLYBAYEV, THE "EAGLE MAN," $100,000 (ABOUT 750,000 TENGE) FOR IT. HE TURNED THE OFFER DOWN, SAYING THE FALCON BELONGED IN KAZAKHSTAN, ITS HOME.

THE AKHAL-TEKE HORSE IS BELIEVED TO BE THE OLDEST PUREBRED HORSE EXTANT. THIS LEGENDARY HORSE HAS BEEN PRIZED FOR CENTURIES FOR ITS UNPARALLELED STAMINA, SPEED, COURAGE AND BEAUTY. IN 1935 AKHAL-TEKES PROVED THEIR EXTRAORDINARY ENDURANCE IN THE FAMOUS 4,300 KILOMETER (2,700 MILE) TREK FROM ASHQABAT TO MOSCOW, COMPLETED IN 84 DAYS. DURING THIS MARCH THEY TRAVELED 360 KILOMETERS (225 MILES) ACROSS THE KARA-KUM DESERT IN 3 DAYS, VIRTUALLY WITHOUT WATER. THIS SPECTACULAR DEMONSTRATION CONVINCED AUTHORITIES TO PROTECT THE PURITY OF THE BREED. IN THE 4TH CENTURY B.C. ALEXANDER THE GREAT WAS STOPPED BY MASSAGETAE WARRIORS MOUNTED ON AKHAL-TEKES, AND IN THE 2ND CENTURY B.C. A CHINESE EMPEROR TRADED SILK FOR THESE "HORSES OF HEAVEN." HERE HORSEMEN TEND TO THEIR HERD IN THE LUGOVOI DISTRICT OF THE ZHAMBYL REGION.

KAZAKH STEPPE HORSES
HAVE LEGENDARY
ENDURANCE AND SERVE
MANY NEEDS. THEY ARE
RIDDEN, RACED, AND USED
IN DRAFT AND ARE ALSO A
SOURCE OF MEAT AND THE
MILK FROM WHICH KUMISS
IS MADE. THEY CAN TRAVEL
200 KILOMETERS (124 MILES)
A DAY WITH EASE AND
SURVIVE TEMPERATURES AS
LOW AS -40 DEGREES
FAHRENHEIT. THIS HERD IS
NEAR BAKANAS OUTSIDE
ALMATY.

"THE BLACK HORSE AT THE FRONT OF THIS HERD IN THE LUGOVOI DISTRICT IS MAYDONLE, THE GRAND-DAUGHTER OF ABSENT, THE MOST SUCCESSFUL HORSE IN OLYMPIC HISTORY. ABSENT WON A GOLD MEDAL, A SILVER MEDAL AND TWO BRONZE MEDALS IN DRESSAGE AT THREE SEPARATE OLYMPIC GAMES IN THE 1960S. MAYDONLE STOOD APART FROM THE HERD AND SIGNALED THE OTHERS WITH A VARIETY OF SOUNDS. WHEN IT WAS TIME TO CROSS THE STREAM, SHE NEIGHED AND LED THEM DOWN THE HILL." – W.E.

A SPINDLY LEGGED COLT FOLLOWS A KAZAKH HORSEMAN TOWARD HOME NEAR THE VILLAGE OF CHILIK IN THE SEVEN RIVERS AREA.

## ORNAMENTATION AND SYMBOLS:
## BEAUTY AND MEANING IN EVERYDAY LIFE

In traditional daily life, even the ordinary Kazakh did not know an unadorned space. Everything around him, beginning with the interior appointments of his yurt, was decorated or "ornamented" by his own or a family member's skilled hands. To adorn something in this manner is to domesticate it – to make it part of one's own cultural universe. Thus, all craft work – from the simplest vessel to a fine blanket, from a horse's harness to items of jewelry – are not only serviceable items of daily life, but also art.

Ornamentation is not simply decoration. It is a special language, and knowing that language opens a path to the nomad's world of art. A dictionary of Kazakh ornamentation would occupy many pages. Among the motifs are cosmic symbols such as the sun, the stars and the crescent moon; geometrical elements such as the triangle, the diamond, the cross and the prehistoric swastika; zoomorphic figurations such as a ram's horn, a bird's wing or a bird's beak, a camel's footprint or

ZHUZIK RING WITH BIRD BEAK DESIGN

a camel's eyes; and botanical representations such as a flower, a leaf or a sprout. All of these elements can be combined in complex constructs that have a philosophical essence comparable to a Buddhist mandala and can be read by cognoscenti like an open book. Kazakh ornamentation is one of humanity's oldest codified symbolic systems comprised of shapes and colors. Thus, the color blue is the symbol of the sky; red represents fire, blood or life itself; green is the symbol of vegetation, spring and beginnings; white represents that which is high or celestial; gold is wisdom or knowledge; and so on.

In Kazakh decorative arts the primary concept is not the opposition between good and evil, but rather the unity of these seemingly contradictory notions, as mentioned earlier. In each ornamental composition can be found a map of the universe, the social group and individuals in unity. Each carpet, for example, is an individual composition, a personal microcosm of the universe that was fashioned by the hardworking hands of a female artisan. Carpets are always outlined by an ornamental border made up of a wave-and-water (*irek* and *su*) motif that represents the worldwide ocean, the basis for life on this earth. The earthly world is, in turn, framed by fish scales and mice tracks; and triangular amulets are framed by the unity of the large rhomboid medallions that symbolize the joining of the male (the triangle pointing upward) and female (the triangle pointing downward) essences.

Inside the rhombus, a symmetrical rosette unites within itself elements representing the two horns of a ram and a bird's wing, which symbolize the world tree – an ornamental formula said to bring fertility and bounty to the owner. At the same time, Kazakh philosophy rejects any single definition for any symbol; each is multilayered and its meaning can change in combination with other symbols. Of particular importance is the triangle and all of the elements that can be linked to it. The magic of the triangle lies in its "trinity" – the union of three worlds in one. According to traditional beliefs, the three sides of the triangle symbolize the fish, the arrow and the bird – representing the three universal elements of water, earth and air. The motif of the ram's horns linked to the triangle represents the fourth element – fire.

The magical connotation of ornaments is self-evident since they "protect" entrances and exits, borders and joined edges, whether of the body, clothing, the yurt or everyday utensils. In the yurt, for example, the patterned strips unite all elements: the lattice framework with the upright support poles, the poles with the *shangïraq*, or roof-hole frame, and the *shashaq bau*, the woven patterned cords with tassels at the end that dangle like rays of a hot sun. Similarly, clothing is decorated at the hem, sleeve and collar, and the edges of headgear and footwear; vessels, indeed most objects, are also decorated: the edges of wooden plates, glasses, the edge of a ladle and the outer side of vessel covers, for example. One can find the same motif on the wooden door of an entryway, on the cupola-like circle of the *shangïraq*, on carpets and on pieces of jewelry. The same ornamentation can be

CARVED WOODEN BOWL

executed in a variety of techniques: carved on wood, etched or brazed onto metal, tooled on leather, rolled or sewn onto felt, embroidered on textile or woven in a pile carpet. It is significant that in Kazakh, the word for decorating or ornamentation is *oyu*, meaning "deepening or carving out," which harkens back to the earliest times of Kazakh life when pictures were carved out of stone. The past has bequeathed us many such monuments – from the petroglyphs that are known around the world, to the famous stone statues called *balbal*, the memorable cupolas of the "cities of the dead," the funerary structures known as *mazar* and the architectural masterpieces of the mosques (*meshit*) and religious schools (*medrese*).

In traditional Kazakh society, applied arts and the production of traditional crafts have been well developed since ancient times. There was also gender specialization in the production of articles required for survival and daily life. Women rolled felt, made woven carpets and mats, and sewed clothing. Men made the

frame of the yurt, furniture, weapons, and harnesses and other accessories for horses. In other words, they worked wood, leather and metal. These activities were interwoven with the annual cycle of economic activities and were combined with daily chores: for women, preparing food and raising children; and for men, tending the animals.

Historically, Kazakh artisans made use of almost every conceivable kind of material available to them. The horns and hooves of domesticated and wild animals were crafted into handles, serving spoons and snuff boxes. Ribs, shoulder-blades, shins and jawbones became carved ornamentation for furniture and details of the yurt. Leather was fashioned into sheepskin coats, headgear, containers, slipcovers and chests, and sewn into horse harnesses, saddles and accessories. Wool and other animal hair was used to make felt, blankets and clothing.

In traditional culture there was no concept of "scraps" or "castaways." Judicious craftsmen and women reused individual fragments of materials, many times in different forms. In almost every Kazakh home you can see quilts (*quraq körpe*) made of scraps of old clothes. Quilts become heirlooms because they relate a family's history from the fragments associated with various members and recall a time when not just the clothing, but the people themselves, were young and handsome.

Most of the applied crafts symbolize the art of the nomads. For me the most vivid examples

of this are the *torsïq*, or kumiss container, that is indispensable for the horseman or traveler on the road; and the *sïrmaq*, or mosaic-like felt rug, that is sure to be found in every yurt.

The *torsïq* is sewn from smooth-grained leather and has horn-like scrolls on each side, a slender throat and a cupola-shaped plug. The frothy kumiss always stays cool and fresh in it, and never spills even if one is riding at a furious gallop. The *sïrmaq* is used to adorn the floor or walls of the yurt, and its decorative motif in the form of a ram's horn is an ornamental formula of Kazakh art.

The art of the bone-carver, or *süyekshi*, has reached a very high level. A variety of traditional wooden products are adorned with carved bone: the headboards of beds; wooden pillows known as *zhastïq aghash*; the support, known as *zhük ayaq*, for holding rolled-up carpets, felts, and pillows at the *tör*, or place of honor; the tops of the lattice framework and roof poles of the yurt; the tops of the churn-staffs for frothing kumiss; and on musical instruments as well.

From a tactile perception, the objects of nomadic daily life are noteworthy for their unique dryness and warmth. Leather products, for example, are warm and dry, as are rugs, textiles, and wood that has been worked, but the warmest of them all is felt. One might even ask through what magical process felt has preserved its warmth for seemingly thousands of years. Centuries-old felt items have been found in good condition by archeologists studying burial sites of the Saka, Hunnish, and Scythian tribes. Well-rolled felt apparently withstands the merciless ravages of time amazingly well and in its own way serves to link nomadic civilization's past with its present.

The preparation of felt is the domain of women. The best wool for making felt is from the fall shearing – the so-called *tiri zhün*, or living wool, that is thick and full compared to the much finer and sparser winter and spring wool. The first step is to clean the wool. The women spread it out on horsehides and beat it with flexible switches. Then they spread the clean, fluffy wool on reed mats, sprinkle it with hot water, and roll it up tight. Five or six women then roll it back and forth with their feet; and to liven up the task, they sing songs to the rhythm of the work. After unrolling the bundle, they roll it up again, this time without a mat. Yet again they roll it back and forth, this time with their elbows to apply more pressure. The hot water and the mechanical rolling of the wool causes it to densely knit together and – there you have it! *Felt!* It becomes so dense and water-repellent that it even can be used to cover the roof of

AYAK KAP, A FELT BAG FOR DISHES

the yurt.

Felt is the basis of many different products, and one of its most important uses is in the making of rugs known as *tekemet* and *sïrmaq*. By placing dyed wool on a partially rolled piece of felt and then resuming the rolling process, a patterned *tekemet* rug is produced in which the borders between the ornamentation and the background are gently blurred.

A unique feature of Kazakh felt rugs is their strict symmetry, which governs both vertical and horizontal lines as well as the functional balance of ornamentation and background. These patterns of symmetry symbolize the coexistence of good and evil, light and dark – the duality of life as derived from the basic religious tenets of Zoroastrianism. This symmetry can be seen most clearly in the mosaic-like carpets called *sïrmaq*. The technique used to make a *sïrmaq* rug is quite simple. Two pieces of felt of contrasting colors are placed atop one another; and with a sharp knife, an ornamental design is cut through both pieces, resulting in two identical cutouts in contrasting colors. The brightly colored cutout is placed on the dark background and the dark one against the brightly colored background. Because of the play of light and how the eye perceives it, the design seems to shimmer or breathe and pulsate, giving the sensation that a world of dialogue is taking place within it.

Woven carpets occupy a significant place in the life of the Kazakhs, although they are found

DETAIL OF FELT RUG

mainly in the south of the country. This is because during this century there has been a more sedentary life there, with stable, stationary looms influenced by the Turkmen. Today, Kazakh carpet weaving has melded the techniques and ornamentation of both of its spheres of influence: the world of nomadic life and the world of the sedentary life. Now there are more than 50 different kinds of Kazakh carpets, among them the so-called "Bukharan carpet" and the "Turkmen carpet." These bear witness to borrowed traits and techniques and mutual influences in carpet weaving among the peoples of Central Asia. These borrowed elements, however, have organically worked themselves into the system of Kazakh ornamentation, which has its own characteristic predominance of certain geometric and zoomorphic motifs.

A particular characteristic of Kazakh woven carpets is their bright, colorful palette. The threads used down until the middle of the 19th century were colored with natural local dyes: boiled concoctions from different variations of leaves, bark, minerals and the roots of trees and plants. Today, modern dyes are also used. Another distinctive feature of

Kazakh woven carpets is the use of sheep's wool as the basic raw material, whereas Uzbek and Turkmen carpets use a mix of wool, cotton and silk because the latter two are more readily available there.

TEXTILE DESIGN

All woven carpets require significant time to create, but vertical looms require a significant amount of space as well. Although carpets woven on a narrow horizontal weaver's beam take up less space, the vertical looms can be erected and disassembled quite easily, which make them more suitable for the nomadic lifestyle. On these frames women weave strips of an unlimited variety of patterns, which they later sew together to form a pileless carpet called *alasha*, or bright-striped carpet. The unique patterned strips are called *basqur*, or main strip, and are used to tie the yurt together on the outside. These are made with a technique that uses woven, piled ornamentation on a pileless background.

Saddlebags and blankets for camels and horses, slipcases for transporting fragile items, and bags hung on the walls of the yurt that are used as sturdy containers for clothing – all of these are

artistic forms of Kazakh carpet weaving or patterned felt-making that create an interior worthy of any museum, art gallery or, for that matter, khan.

Leather crafts also occupy an important place in the Kazakh spectrum of applied arts. Kazakhs are among the world's best in making products from the skins of domesticated and wild animals. They have become masters at preparing a hide so it takes on the softest, most supple quality. The process consists of removing the fat from a hide with salt, drying the hide and carefully softening it in numerous steps with sour milk (*ayran*) or dried milk solids (*qurt*). Once it is suitably pliable and supple, it can be used to make fur coats, footwear or even dishware.

From horsehides, containers called *saba* are sewn. These are nearly as high as a person and are used to ferment mare's milk to make kumiss, or camel's milk to make *shubat*. The skin from a camel's neck is used to make *süyretpe*, containers that hold two buckets of milk. Goatskins taken whole are made into containers called *mes* that are used to transport milk products. Milk pails, or *könek*, are made from the hides of oxen and camels. (Nomads say that when one milks a camel, the sound of milk spurting into a *könek* calms the animal, whereas the sound it makes in a metal pail frightens it, causing the camel to stop giving milk.)

Warm sheepskin coats – with the fur on the inside, a facing of velvet or plain cloth on the outside, and a high collar that can

cover the head – are indispensable during Kazakh winters. Fox coats would be worn by aristocrats or the wealthy, but were inaccessible

19TH-CENTURY **SHAPAN** WITH SILK EMBROIDERY

to the typical nomad. Yet a fox hat (a *qulaqshïn* or *tïmaq*) – with a flap covering the nape of the neck and two flaps tied under the chin – was not just a dream, but a reality for most Kazakhs.

Kazakhs also had marvelous felts of camel hair, similar to the most supple suede, out of which a warm robe called a *shapan* was sewn. The *shapan*, with its wide folds like a cape and its long arms, was the daily attire of the livestock herder. A *shapan* could also be made from homespun cloth or from store-bought satin, and a quilted wool lining would be sewn inside.

The traditional leather belt, with silver buckle and silver pendants, held the man's costume together, but had social significance as well. As was also the case with headgear, the cut and adornment of the belt symbolized the age, social status and tribal affiliation of its owner. Tradition categorically forbids giving either belt or headgear to anyone else because the belt binds a man's middle, and thus his navel, or being; fortune and luck would abandon the person who did. Thus, only belts and hats that were brand new could be given as gifts. When not worn, the belt and headgear were stored high up in a place of honor in the yurt or on a special hanger, the *adalbaqan*, used to display clothing.

The zenith of Kazakh artisans is often considered to be the wedding costume of the bride, which brings together all forms of traditional arts. As in many other cultures, the bride's dress of white silk symbolizes her purity. Over the dress she wears a *qamzol* – a fitted, red-velvet vest embroidered with silver thread. A silver belt with precious jewels affixed complements an assortment of silver bracelets, signet rings and other rings. Hanging from the collar of her dress on a chain or decorative string is a silver breastplate or embroidery called *öngirshe*, and coral or pearl beads. Silver decorations on bone, known as *sholpï*, are threaded onto velvet ribbons; these, along with money tied with silk cords and pendants in the shape of a fish or a crescent moon, hang down the back to symbolically protect the bride's spine and lower back. Her headdress serves as a symbol of the bridal ceremony and is known as the *säukele*. With a value placed at tens of

camels, it was passed on from generation to generation or gathered piece by piece from the time of a daughter's birth. The shape of the *säukele* has sexual connotations. It is a cone that stands about half a meter or one-and-a-half feet high. Made of felt or velvet or brocade wrapped around a rigid frame, it is decorated with silver and precious jewels, hanging pendants and topped with a sheaf of eagle or owl feathers. It looks very much like the crown of the Golden Warrior from the Issïq burial mound. The variety of the *säukele* and the many meanings of its composition are fascinating and almost endless.

It is worth mentioning here that the most valuable decorative objects are prepared by an artisan jeweler known as a *zerger*. This craftsman is a master of metalwork who combines the skills of a smith and a jeweler. His workshop is a secretive, if not a mystical place, because the combination of working with fire and liquefied metals is considered to be the work of a cultural innovator not unlike Prometheus. Moreover, the products of the *zerger*, filled with blessings and good wishes, brought happiness and good fortune to young families.

The creations of the *zergers* are striking for their simple yet sophisticated execution, comparable to fine art in the so-called "animal style" of the ancient nomads of Eurasia. Bracelets with cornelian settings through which fine chains are linked with three rings – once again paralleling the Upper, Middle and Lower Worlds

– often are fashioned in the form of a *qusmurun*, or bird's beak; a *qusqanat*, or bird's wing; or a yurt. These are an essential part of a bride's dowry. Even during World War II when the Communist regime undertook mass confiscation of Kazakh silver under the guise of "voluntary" contributions to aid in its war efforts, mothers buried silver jewelry for their daughters. Such an offense was punishable by death, which means that these mothers could not imagine their daughters' future marriage without this traditional means of protection, blessings and hope.

Even in an overview such as this, the myriad applications of ornamentation and adornment in Kazakh culture – from dwellings to furniture, from utensils to weapons and from ceremonial dress to winter clothing – quickly becomes evident. It is not an exaggeration to state that in the Circle of Life, from birth to death, the cycle of a Kazakh's being is spent in a world of beauty whose elements are repeated through colors, shapes, symbols and signs of the natural world. In other words, the world of nature is perceived and organized into everyday life by the very same laws as the world of man, and vice versa. This is the essence of the sense of comfort, protection and eternity that was so necessary in the constantly changing life of the nomad.

17TH-CENTURY SILVER RING FROM OTRAR

NOMADIC DWELLINGS AS DEPICTED BY A MEDIEVAL IRANIAN ARTIST.

ORNAMENTATION IN DAILY LIFE: "TO ADORN SOMETHING IN THIS MANNER IS TO DOMESTICATE IT –
TO MAKE IT PART OF ONE'S CULTURAL UNIVERSE." — A.K.

APPAREL AND HATS ARE A
DISTINCTIVE PART OF THE
NATIONAL COSTUME THAT
INDICATE THE AGE, GENDER
AND STATUS OF THE WEARER.
THESE HATS COME FROM
THE VARIOUS CLANS AND
TRIBES OF THE THREE
KAZAKH HORDES, DATING
TO ANTIQUITY. THIS
COLLECTION IS A GOOD
EXAMPLE OF HOW EACH
OF THE GROUPS EXPRESS
RICH AND UNIQUE
CHARACTERISTICS OF THE
KAZAKH PERSONALITY.
CENTRAL STATE MUSEUM, ALMATY.

A KEY TO THESE HATS
APPEARS ON THE NEXT PAGE.

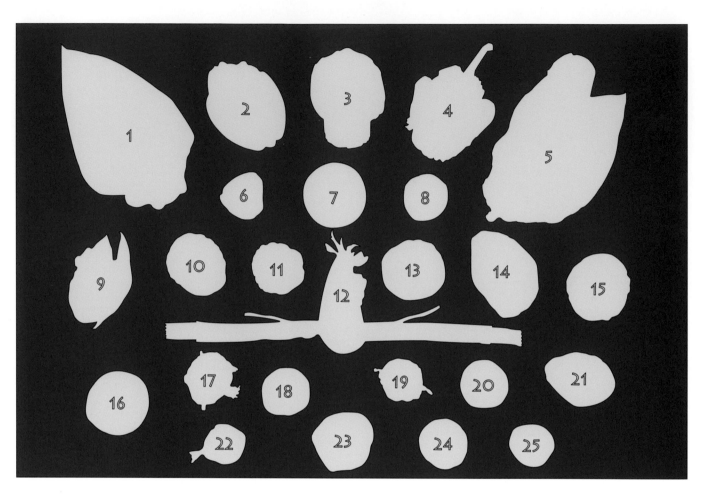

KEY FOR NUMBERS:

1, 5      **KIMESHEK** – LADIES' HAT THAT COVERS HEAD, SHOULDERS AND BACK; NO VEIL.

2, 4      **TÏMAQ** – POPULAR MEN'S WINTER HAT.

3, 6, 23      **KASABA** – YOUNG LADIES' HAT EMBROIDERED WITH GOLD AND SILVER.

8, 18, 20      **TAKIYA** – SMALL FABRIC HAT MANDATORILY WORN BY MEN UNDER AN OUTER HAT.

22, 24, 25

17, 19      **TAKIYA** – WORN BY WOMEN, BUT NOT MANDATORY.

10, 13, 15      **BORIK** – FUR HAT WORN BY MEN YEAR-ROUND.

7, 11      **BORIK** – YOUNG LADIES' VERSION OF SAME HAT.

9, 14      **AIYRKALPAK** – MEN'S TALL HAT FOR NOTABLES; WORN ON TOP OF CONE-SHAPED HAT WITH FUR TRIM.

16, 21      **KALPAK** – MEN'S SUMMER FELT HAT.

12      **SÄUKELE** – CEREMONIAL HAT WORN BY WOMEN FIRST AT THEIR WEDDING, THEN ON SPECIAL OCCASIONS OR WHEN HONORED GUESTS VISIT.

THIS DETAIL IS FROM A PILE CARPET CALLED
**TOKTYKLEM**. IT IS A 20TH-CENTURY CREATION
FROM SHYMKENT IN SOUTHERN KAZAKHSTAN.
KASTEYEV MUSEUM OF FINE ARTS, ALMATY.

NURZIPHA ZHANGAZIYEVA WEAVES A MODERN-STYLE
CARPET, BASED ON ANCIENT KAZAKH PETROGLYPHS,
ON A VERTICAL LOOM AT THE TAMGA CARPET FACTORY
IN FABRICHNY IN SOUTHEASTERN KAZAKHSTAN.

FATIMA ADAI DEMONSTRATES HER STRAP-WEAVING
TECHNIQUE AT HER HOME IN AKTAU. HER FAMILY
MOVED TO IRAN AFTER THE 1917 OCTOBER
REVOLUTION AND SHE LEARNED WEAVING THERE.
RETURNING TO KAZAKHSTAN IN 1997, SHE MERGED
HER PERSIAN TECHNIQUE WITH HER KAZAKH
DESIGN TO CREATE A BEAUTIFUL, NEW HYBRID STYLE.

MASTER FELT-MAKERS ZEKEN ZARYKPAI-KYZY SYGAYEVA AND KAINEKE ZARYKPAI-KYZY KANAPYANOVA BEGIN
THE FELT-MAKING PROCESS IN THE VILLAGE OF ABAI NOT FAR FROM ALMATY.

THE PICTURES ON THESE PAGES DEPICT THE MAKING OF FELT – USED IN A SEEMINGLY ENDLESS NUMBER OF APPLICATIONS SUCH
AS CARPETS, HATS, YURT INSULATION COVERS, BOOT LINERS, ETC. – FROM SHEEP'S WOOL. THE TECHNIQUE SEEMS RATHER SIM-
PLE, THE RESULT ALMOST MAGICAL. THERE ARE A NUMBER OF VARIATIONS, BUT ONE COMMON METHOD IS DEPICTED HERE:
WOOL IS PULLED TO LENGTHEN AND RELAX THE FIBERS, THEN BEATEN WITH SWITCHES TO CLEAN AND FURTHER RELAX THEM.
THE WOOL IS THEN LAID OUT IN SMALL HANDFULS TO FORM THE ENVISIONED DESIGN ON A CHI, OR REED MAT. HOT WATER
IS POURED ONTO THE FELT AND THE MAT IS ROLLED UP INTO A TIGHT BUNDLE LIKE A JELLY ROLL. IT IS ROLLED AND UNROLLED
A NUMBER OF TIMES, AND THE MAGIC HAPPENS AS THE FIBERS BEGIN TO LOCK TOGETHER. MORE HOT WATER IS APPLIED AND
THE FELT IS THEN ROLLED AND UNROLLED WITHOUT THE CHI MAT. THE MORE TIMES THE FELT IS ROLLED UP, THE TIGHTER
AND FINER THE FINISHED FELT BECOMES.

VILLAGE LADIES WORK TOGETHER TO MAKE FINE FELT IN SHIELI IN THE QÏZÏLORDA REGION.

THIS FINE FELT RUG IS A GOOD EXAMPLE OF A 20TH-CENTURY **TEKEMET**, AS THEY ARE CALLED.
IT WAS MADE IN SOUTHERN KAZAKHSTAN BY BIBI AISHA ROMANOVA.
KASTEYEV MUSEUM OF FINE ARTS, ALMATY.

WITH EXPERIENCED AND
WEATHERED HANDS, ZEKEN
ZARYKPAI-KYZY SYGAYEVA
AND KAINEKE ZARYKPAI-
KYZY KANAPYANOVA
PREPARE TO WORK THEIR
FELT-MAKING MAGIC AS
THEY TIGHTLY ROLL UP THE
PREPARED WOOL FIBERS.

A HANDMADE CARPET OF DYED WOOL TAKES SHAPE ON A HORIZONTAL LOOM THROUGH THE ARTISTRY OF BEIBIT IKHANOVA, LEFT, AND ZHANILYA BEKTASOVA IN THE VILLAGE OF SHIELI.

AMANGUL IKHANOVA WEAVES AN ARTISTIC PATTERN ON A LOOM WITH HER DAUGHTERS KURALAI, 16, AND MERUERT, 13, AT HER STUDIO IN THE ARTISTS UNION BUILDING IN ALMATY.

ZAKIYA AKAI-KYZY IS A PRACTICING ATTORNEY BESIDES BEING A MASTER EMBROIDERER AND **CHI** ARTIST. HER WORK IS A GOOD EXAMPLE OF CROSS-CULTURAL INFLUENCES DUE TO THE TIME SHE SPENT IN MONGOLIA. HERE SHE WORKS ON A **TUSKIIZ** USING A CHAIN STITCH CALLED "THE TRACE OF THE MOUSE." A **TUSKIIZ** IS A WALL-HANGING THAT CAN ALSO BE USED AS A DECORATIVE COVERING.

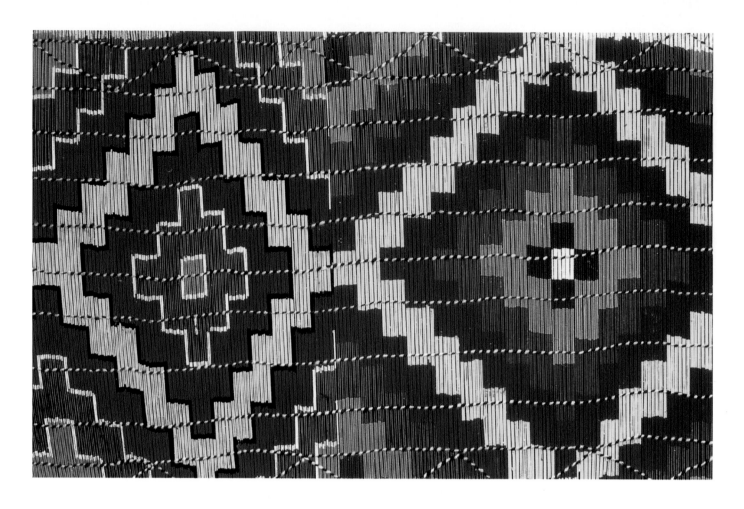

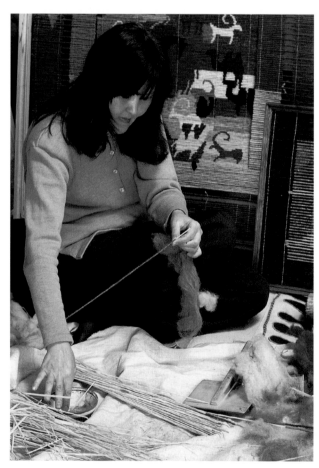

DYED WOOL IS WRAPPED AROUND REEDS, THEN STITCHED TOGETHER TO MAKE **CHI** MATS TO ADORN THE EXTERIOR WALLS OF THE YURT. THIS ONE WAS CREATED BY ZAKIYA AKAI-KYZY.

RAIGUL AKHMETZHANOVA LEARNED TRADITIONAL **CHI** MAKING (REEDS WRAPPED WITH WOOL) FROM ELDERLY KAZAKH WOMEN. SHE USES THE AGE-OLD TECHNIQUE TO EXPRESS HER MODERN ART.

ZHANGIR UMBETOV WORKS IN VARIOUS ARTISTIC MEDIA. HE HAS CREATED THIS CEREMONIAL HAT FOR A YOUNG LADY, USING OWL FEATHERS AS A PLUME FOR THEIR SACRED POWER.

THE ALMATY STUDIO OF
ARTISTS AMANGUL
IKHANOVA AND ZHANGIR
UMBETOV REFLECTS THE
PROFUSION OF ACTIVITIES
AND MEDIA THEY WORK IN:
WEAVING, PAINTING,
SCULPTING AND JEWELRY
MAKING. THE STUDIO ALSO
RECREATES A MICROCOSM
OF KAZAKH CULTURE, WITH
THE MUSICAL **DOMBRA**
INSTRUMENTS AND THE
SACRED WOLF HIDE HANGING
ON THE WALL AND THE
**DASTARQAN** LAID OUT WITH
FOOD. THIS HUSBAND-AND-
WIFE TEAM HAVE CREATED
A UNIQUE KAZAKH ART
FORM, CALLED **KÜSHKON**, IN
WHICH THEY DYE LEATHER
AND CREATE A WORK THAT
IS BOTH SCULPTURE AND
PAINTING. THE CONCEPTS
FOR MOST OF THEIR PIECES
ARE DRAWN FROM
TENGRISM, SHAMANISM,
SUFISM AND
ZOROASTRIANISM. THEY
ARE BOTH FROM THE
QÏZÏLORDA REGION.

THIS CORAL **TUSKIIZ** WAS MADE BY MARIYA ILAKOVA IN 1913. ITS INTRICATE DESIGN INCLUDES VELVET, SILK, CORAL, TURQUOISE, CORNELIAN, AGATE AND EMBROIDERY. IT INCLUDES PIECES OF WEDDING JEWELRY THAT WERE SOWN INTO THE TEXTILE AFTER THE MARRIAGE CEREMONY. A **TUSKIIZ** WAS MADE BY THE BRIDE BEFORE THE WEDDING AND HUNG IN AN HONORARY PLACE SO THE GROOM'S RELATIVES COULD APPRAISE HER SKILL. **TUSKIIZ** ARE USED AS WALL DECORATIONS AND TO COVER STACKED FUTONS. KASTEYEV MUSEUM OF FINE ARTS, ALMATY.

LEATHER ARTIST SEKEN NURGALIYEV LEARNED HIS CRAFT FROM HIS FATHER, ZHUMAGAZY (AT CENTER, REAR), A MASTER LEATHER CRAFTSMAN IN THE VILLAGE OF SHIBER-AUL. A TERRITORIAL GOVERNOR, WHOSE PRIZED FALCON HAD LOST PART OF ITS TALON, ASKED ZHUMAGAZY TO HELP RESTORE IT WITH HIS LEATHER CRAFT. HIS WORK WAS SO SUCCESSFUL THAT THE GOVERNOR OFFERED HIM HIS DAUGHTER'S HAND IN MARRIAGE. ZHUMAGAZY ACCEPTED. IN THIS PHOTO, SEKEN IS WORKING ON A REPRESENTATION OF ZHAMBÏL, THE MASTER OF IMPROVISED POETRY (1846-1945), WHOSE THEMES WERE STRUGGLES BETWEEN GOOD AND EVIL, AND COMPASSION FOR PEOPLE'S MISFORTUNES.

THE OBJECTS IN THIS TABLEAU IN THE ALMATY STUDIO OF ARTISTS AMANGUL IKHANOVA AND ZHANGIR UMBETOV ARE
EXAMPLES OF TRADITIONAL KAZAKH LIFE: HANGING ON THE WALL ARE, FROM LEFT, A TOTEMIC WOLF HIDE; A LEATHER
**KESE KAP**, WHICH IS USED TO STORE CUPS AND BOWLS AND IS TIED TO THE SADDLE; A HORSE TAIL; A FOX HIDE;
A SMALL, DECORATIVE FELT STORAGE BAG, AND TWO **DOMBÏRAS**, ALSO CALLED **DOMBRAS**, THE TRADITIONAL MUSICAL
INSTRUMENT. STANDING ON THE TABLE ARE, FROM LEFT, THREE **TORSÏQS**, WHICH ARE FLASKS TO HOLD KUMISS, THE
FERMENTED MARE'S MILK DRINK; A LEATHER BELT WITH SILVER AND TURQUOISE DECORATION; A BRASS MORTAR AND PESTLE;
A KUMISS CUP; PITCHERS FOR OIL; AND AN IMPORTED RUSSIAN SAMOVAR FOR TEA. A **TUSKIIZ** HANGS ON THE WALL.

THE **DOMBRA**, LIKE THIS ONE BEING CRAFTED BUT NOT YET ASSEMBLED, IS A TWO-STRINGED INSTRUMENT THAT IS STRUMMED AND PLUCKED. IT IS USED TO ACCOMPANY SONGS AND ALSO TO PERFORM INSTRUMENTAL MELODIES CALLED **KÜYS**. THE **DOMBRA** IS THE INSEPARABLE COMPANION OF THE NOMAD.

ZHOLAOUSHY TURDUGULOV IS A MASTER INSTRUMENT MAKER WHO IS ALSO THE GRAND-PRIZE WINNER IN PERFORMANCE WITH THE **DOMBÏRA**, OR **DOMBRA**, AS IT IS ALSO CALLED. HERE HE CHECKS THE SOUND BOARD OF A NEW ONE HE IS MAKING OUT OF TRADITIONAL APPLE WOOD IN HIS WORKSHOP AT THE DEPARTMENT OF APPLIED ARTS OF ALMATY UNIVERSITY WHERE HE IS A PROFESSOR. AITMUKHAMBET TEZHEKENOV, A MUSICIAN, HAS STOPPED BY TO CHECK ON A **DOMBÏRA** BEING MADE FOR HIM.

A STUDENT WORKS ON CREATING THE DESIGN ON A MUSICAL INSTRUMENT CALLED A **QÏL QOBÏZ** AT THE APPLIED ARTS DEPARTMENT AT ALMATY UNIVERSITY. THE **QOBÏZ** IS ONE OF THE WORLD'S OLDEST INSTRUMENTS AND IS CONSIDERED TO BE THE ANCESTOR OF EUROPEAN BOWED INSTRUMENTS, INCLUDING THE VIOLIN.

THE BELT IN ANCIENT TIMES WAS THE SIGN OF A WARRIOR, STRICTLY DESIGNATING RANK. OVER THE CENTURIES IT TOOK ON ADDITIONAL MEANINGS FOR SHEPHERDS AND HUNTERS AND WAS SOON WORN BY BOTH MEN AND WOMEN. BELTS WERE SIMILAR TO JEWELRY AND TEXTILES IN THAT THEIR ORNAMENTATION CARRIED LAYERS OF MEANING AND SYMBOLISM. A CONTAINED CIRCLE REPRESENTS THE UNIVERSE, FOR EXAMPLE, AND HOLDS SACRED MEANING. THE BELT COULD GUARD AGAINST THE EVIL EYE, OR BE GIVEN AS AN AWARD IN HORSE RACING. SILVER WAS THE PREFERRED METAL AND DESIGN MOTIFS RANGED FROM THE ZOOMORPHIC, SUCH AS RAM'S HORNS, TO THE BOTANICAL, SUCH AS TULIP BLOSSOMS OR ROSETTE PETALS.

EAST KAZAKHSTAN REGIONAL HISTORICAL MUSEUM, OSKEMEN.

ZHARGAK TON (MAN'S FUR COAT). 19TH CENTURY. CHAMOIS, SILK-STITCH EMBROIDERY. ZHAMBYL REGION, SOUTHERN KAZAKHSTAN.

CENTRAL STATE MUSEUM, ALMATY.

FROM LEFT, **ZHARGAK SHALBAR** (MAN'S TROUSERS). 1886. CHAMOIS, SILK-STITCH EMBROIDERY. ZHAUMEN DISTRICT, SOUTHERN KAZAKHSTAN; **KEMER BELDIK** (MAN'S BELT). EARLY 20TH CENTURY. LEATHER, SILVER PLATE; **ETIK** (MAN'S BOOTS). EARLY 20TH CENTURY. CHAMOIS, HANDMADE. TALDYKORGAN REGION, EASTERN KAZAKHSTAN.

CENTRAL STATE MUSEUM, ALMATY.

SENSEN TON (MAN'S FUR COAT). EARLY 20TH CENTURY. SHEEPSKIN COAT LINED WITH FUR, COLORED WITH POMEGRANATE ARIL. MANGYSHLAK, WESTERN KAZAKHSTAN. CENTRAL STATE MUSEUM, ALMATY.

ISHIK (WOMAN'S FUR COAT). EARLY 19TH CENTURY. SWAN'S DOWN COVERED WITH SILK AND VELVET. FRINGED SILK SHAWL. THE COAT BELONGED TO THE SISTER OF CHOKAN VALIKHANOV (SHOQAN UÄLIKHANOV), THE EXPLORER, TRAVELER AND SCHOLAR WHO WAS A GRANDSON OF THE LAST KHAN OF THE MIDDLE HORDE. CENTRAL STATE MUSEUM, ALMATY.

THESE REPRODUCTIONS OF BATTLE-AXES DATING FROM THE 16TH TO THE 17TH CENTURIES ARE EXAMPLES OF THE AUTHENTICISM ACHIEVED IN THE MEDIEVAL WEAPONS CRAFTED BY THE KOULMANOV BROTHERS.

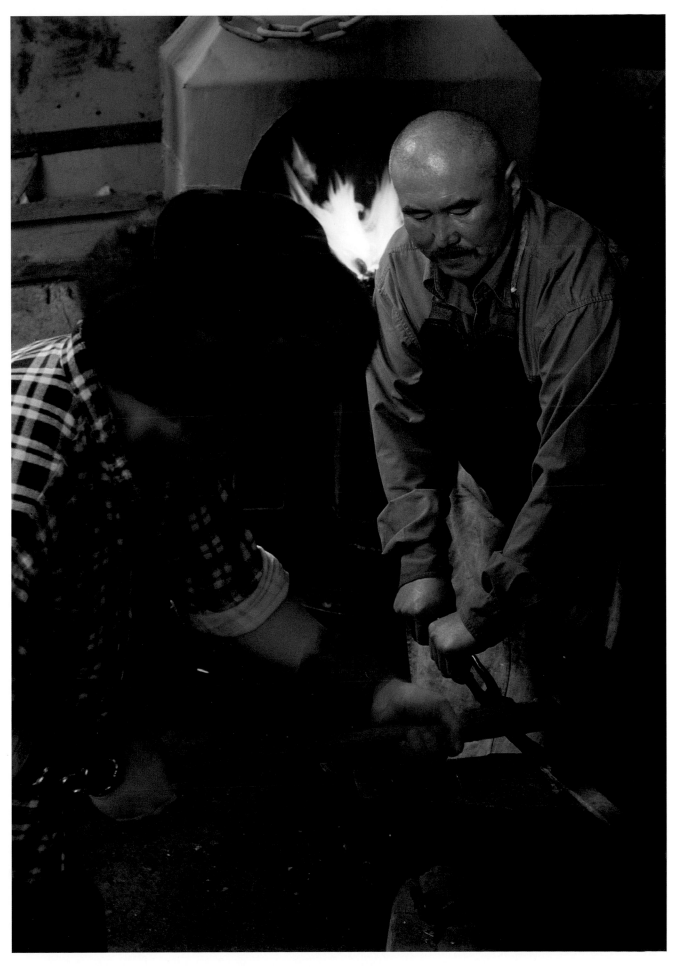

THE KOULMANOV BROTHERS – TOURSOUNJAN, MACHMOUD AND AYTBERGEN – ARE MASTER METALSMITHS AND HISTORIANS. AFTER METICULOUS RESEARCH, THEY USE ORIGINAL METHODS AND MATERIALS TO RECREATE PERIOD WEAPONS, SADDLES AND STANDARDS AT THEIR WORKSHOP IN ALMATY. THEIR ATTENTION TO DETAIL EXTENDS TO THEIR FORGING THE METAL THEY USE IN THEIR CRAFT.

THIS REPRODUCTION OF AN
8TH CENTURY B.C. WAR MASK
CREATED BY THE KOULMANOV
BROTHERS IS IN THE STYLE
OF SKIFF AND MASSAGETAE
TRIBES, PART OF THE SCYTHIAN
FEDERATION THAT POPULATED
CENTRAL ASIA. THE ORIGINAL
IS IN A MOSCOW MUSEUM.
THE FACE IS HINGED AT THE
FOREHEAD SO THE WARRIOR
COULD ADJUST IT THE
MOMENT HE ENGAGED THE
ENEMY. THE KOULMANOV
BROTHER HERE LOOKS AS
THOUGH THE MASK MIGHT
HAVE BEEN MADE JUST FOR
HIM.

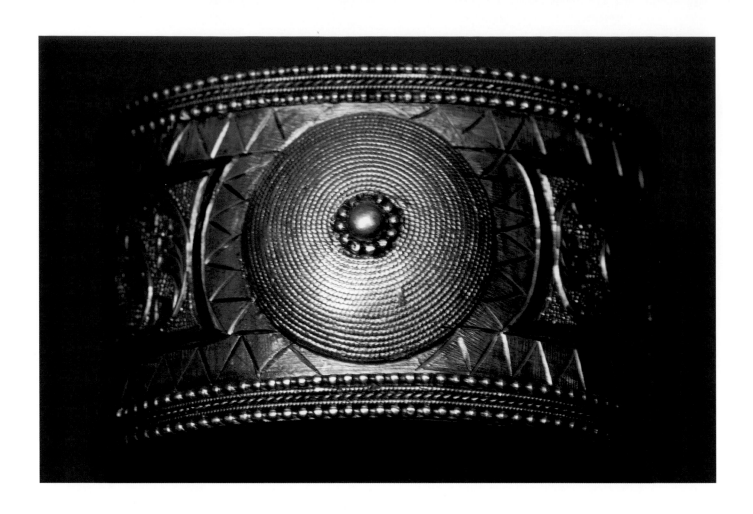

BILEZIK (BRACELET). 19TH CENTURY. SILVER, NIELLO (A BLACK ALLOY INLAY), ENGRAVING AND FILIGREE.
AQTOBE, NORTHWESTERN KAZAKHSTAN. CENTRAL STATE MUSEUM, ALMATY.

BILEZIK (BRACELET). 19TH CENTURY. SILVER, CORNELIAN, GILT, GRAIN, STAMPING AND EMBOSSING. WESTERN KAZAKHSTAN.
CENTRAL STATE MUSEUM, ALMATY.

SYRGA (EARRING). 20TH CENTURY. SILVER, CORAL, TURQUOISE AND GLASS. CENTRAL KAZAKHSTAN.
KASTEYEV MUSEUM OF FINE ARTS, ALMATY.

TUIME (BUTTON). 19TH CENTURY. SILVER, GILT, GRAIN, STAMPING AND EMBOSSING. WESTERN KAZAKHSTAN.
CENTRAL STATE MUSEUM, ALMATY.

**TUIME** (BUTTON). EARLY 20TH CENTURY. SILVER, GLASS, STAMPING AND BUCKLING.

CENTRAL STATE MUSEUM, ALMATY.

KUDAGI ZHUZIK (SIGNET RING FOR MOTHERS-IN-LAW). 19TH CENTURY. SILVER, GLASS, GILT, STAMPING AND EMBOSSING.
THE **TUMAR** (TRIANGLE DESIGN) POINTING UPWARD IS THE MALE SYMBOL; DOWNWARD IT REPRESENTS THE FEMALE.
ORAL, WESTERN KAZAKHSTAN.   KASTEYEV MUSEUM OF FINE ARTS, ALMATY.

# FINE ARTS:
## PERSONAL VISIONS OF KAZAKHSTAN

The October Revolution of 1917 that began in far-off St. Petersburg had resounding consequences across the steppes of Central Asia as well. The resulting upheaval posed a tremendous challenge for the Kazakh people and their culture. Under the banner of creating a new socialist culture – which had a single "correct," i.e. Russian, face – the rulers of the Soviet Empire established a Union of Artists in Kazakhstan in1933 and a School of Art in 1938. The latter became a "forge of cadres," an alma mater for a new generation of artists and sculptors who continued their education at the art academies of Moscow, Leningrad, Kharkov and other Russian cities, then called "All-Union" centers of art.

There was in this a bold task of incomprehensible proportions: rapid adaptation by the nomads of European art in all its contemporary forms. During the years of the forced collectivization and sedentarization, during the time of famine and the ruin of civil war, a new type of art was instilled in the bosom of Kazakh culture that quickly became the reality of the 1920s and 1930s.

This was possible because traditional folk art over the centuries, which though predominantly ornamental and symbolic, is also deeply philosophical, and laid the groundwork for a new stage in its historical development. By using their trained, precise gazes and their steady hands, the master artists cultivated new uses of texture, lines, color and form. Artists used their talents and responded to their new obligation brilliantly, promoting from among their ranks those who successfully assimilated the technology of the new arts and depicted the new national spirit in painting, sculpture, graphic art and architecture.

Under pressure from the doctrine of socialist realism and strict ideological control, the founders of Kazakh painting Äbilxan Küsteev (1904-1973) and Äubäkir Ïsmailov (born 1913) directed their attention first to landscapes, portraiture and scenes of daily life, which for a long time appeared to be the basic genres of all painters.

The natural beauty of the motherland and the infinite variety of its landscapes became the major theme of many artists. Mountains occupied a significant place in their work, echoing the traditional worldview of their sacredness – the spurs of the Tien Shan such as the Alatau and Qaratau, covered eternally with snow – symbols of the loftiness of the human spirit, eternity and sacred knowledge. The mountains served almost as a reference point for orientation in life and gave the starting coordinates for existence. But landscapes were rarely just a depiction of nature – as a rule, at the heart of a canvas was a yurt, gardens, children, animals or scenes of nomadic life.

The artists themselves knew Kazakh life thoroughly and were representatives of this culture, and they glorified it in all its variety. Portraits captured not just the people of that time but also their clothing, daily life and occupations. It would be interesting and productive at some point to analyze these pictures from an ethnographic point of view. In the meantime, it can be said that Kazakh figurative art of the middle of the 20th century chronicles its own time with all of its positive and negative characteristics.

Viewing the works of the 1940s and 1950s, one senses a sentimental feeling, a nostalgia, a period in which the painters of these canvases were avoiding the horrible truth of life and attempting to instill a hopeful yearning for the eternal ideas of happiness, equality and prosperity. This tone is akin in some ways to the work of the American painter, Norman Rockwell, who despite idealizing his subjects, correctly captured the national mood of his time.

An important place in Kazakh painting of this period is occupied by the work of the first modern female artist, Aysha Ghalimbayeva, whose lyrical vision is clearly imprinted on post-war art. She participated in the production of such popular and well-loved artistic films as *The Songs of Abay* (1945), *The Legend about Love* (1953), *Brave Girl* (1955), and others. Her album of paintings entitled "Kazakh National Costumes," which she completed following many years of research, serves today as an indispensable source for Kazakh ethnography.

Gülfäyrüz Ismailova, who created a wonderful oil portrait of the opera singer Kulyash Bayseitova in the role of the epic heroine Qïz-Zhibek, is well known not just because of her many paintings, but also because of her work in cinema. All three – the historical Qïz-Zhibek, Kulyash who portrayed her, and Gülfäyrüz who captured the two of them on canvas – became symbols of Kazakh beauty, irresistible charm, femininity and faithfulness. This uninterrupted chain of incarnations and reincarnations of the epic ideal in contemporary life is yet another characteristic feature of Kazakh culture, in which art is life and life is art.

The Russian artist Evgeniy Sidorkin (1930-1982), who fell in love with the beautiful Ismailova, devoted his life to representing the charm of Kazakh women and to recreating the heroes and heroines of Kazakh epic history. The historical novel *The Way of Abay*, by Mukhtar Äuezov, was republished many times with drawings by Sidorkin. Thanks to this artist the characters of the novel acquired unforgettable faces that are accepted today almost as historical documents. Also widely known are a series of his illustrations of Kazakh epics, drawings and pictures that occupy their own worthy place in the history of contemporary Kazakh art.

The building of cities – first of all Almaty, capital of Soviet Kazakhstan – was a fundamental aspect of the transformation of nomadic culture toward an urban culture. This task was carried out to a great extent after the Great Patriotic War (World War II) by a young band of architects headed by Malbaghar Mendikulov (1909-1986), one of the founders of the architectural school of

Kazakhstan. He designed many of the buildings and monuments that became symbols of Almaty. Among them are the Palace of Weddings; the Qarlïghash (Swallow) Café, a city-center spot beloved by young people; and the architectural aspects of the monuments to Zhambïl Zhabayev and Mukhtar Äuezov by sculptors Kh. Naurïzbayev (b. 1925) and T. Dosmaghambetov (b. 1940).

Official propaganda attached great significance to monumental sculpture as a means of ideological education. Thanks to this, practically the entire territory of Kazakhstan was literally strewn with copies of sculptures and busts of Marx, Engels, Lenin and Stalin in sanctioned poses, always with the same expression on their faces. History has delivered its own verdict of this genre of "art." Fortunately, the young sculptors of Kazakhstan also devoted a significant part of their creativity to other works that have rightfully entered into the cultural heritage of the nation. They restored – on the basis of old photographs and conversations with contemporaries and relatives – portraits and sculptures of figures who constituted the pride and historical memory of the nation. Among them are sculptures of the brilliant scholar, Chokan Valikhanov (in Kazakh, Shoqan Uälikhanov, 1835-1865); the great enlightener and founder of modern Kazakh written literature, Abay Qunanbay (1845-1904); the famed poet Zhambïl Zhabayev (1846-1945); and fighters for Kazakh independence, Makhambat Ötemisov (1803-1845) and Amankeldi

Imanov (1873-1919).

All of these figures are symbols of the Kazakh spirit, its finest names worthy of representing Kazakhs in the world arena. Without understanding their contributions to national culture it is impossible to understand why their images occupy such a place in the contemporary arts of the Kazakhs. Thus Chokan Valikhanov – a great-grandson of Khan Abïlay, a founder of Kazakh statehood; and grandson of the last khan of the Middle Horde – was the first Kazakh Orientalist, historian, geographer and ethnographer. He received an outstanding education at the Omsk cadet academy and knew Arabic, Persian, Uighur, Chaghatay and Russian; he participated in ethnographic expeditions and was a member of the Imperial Russian Geographic Society in St. Petersburg. His works, now published in five volumes, are dedicated to the history and culture of all the peoples of Central Asia. He is one of the first scholars to have transcribed the Great Epics of the Steppe (the Kyrgyz *Manas*, the Kazakh tales *Kozï-Körpesh and Bayan-Sulu, Edigey,* and others) and annotated them, thus raising the scholarly and philosophical understanding of the features of nomadic culture to the highest level. From the pages of his articles and books emerge a world structured and organized according to the laws of beauty, full of meaning, memory and heroism. This unique scholar, who united East and West in his short life, laid the foundation for an intercultural dialogue filled with pain, courage and hope. His works have not lost their meaning and to this day are cited by scholars in Kazakhstan and abroad. For Kazakhs, Chokan Valikhanov epitomizes scholarly knowledge and investigation. Suffice it to say that the monument to Chokan Chingiz-ulï Valikhanov stands at the entrance to the National Academy of Sciences of Kazakhstan in Almaty, and institutes, schools and streets are named in his honor.

No less significant is the towering figure of Abay. His life, poetry and philosophy have defined the spiritual contours of Kazakh culture for almost a century and a half. Abay was a great statesman who clearly perceived the tragedy of that pivotal period in the history of his people. He saw that Kazakh hopes for salvation lay in learning, education and acquisition of world culture. As a connoisseur of both Eastern and Western poetry, Abay translated into Kazakh the poems of Goethe and Byron, Pushkin and Lermontov, and popularized the works of Spenser, Spinoza and Darwin. The poems of Abay, as well as his philosophical and romantic lyrics, were widely known in the steppes, and excerpts of his translations of *Eugene Onegin* by Aleksandr Pushkin became an organic component of Kazakh sung folklore. (Abay himself composed melodies to his songs and poetic translations.)

Abay was the organizer and judge of musical poetry contests in his own village. He was a master at playing the *dombïra* (pronounced and commonly spelled "dombra") and was also a gifted composer who wrote songs for the instrument

as well. The 1960 monument to Abay in Almaty became a must-see landmark of the southern capital, and widely known abroad. The celebrated 1944 opera *Abay* was dedicated to the centennial of his birth by composers Akhmet Zhubanov and Latif Khamidi; the libretto, by Mukhtar Äuezov, is a classic of modern Kazakh literature. The historical novel,

MEMORIAL TO ABAY QUNANBAY, SHAKARIM QUDAYBERDIEV, AND MUKHTAR ÄUEZOV

ÄUEZOV MAUSOLEUM AT BORLI-AUL

*The Way of Abay*, written in four volumes between 1942 and 1956 by Mukhtar Äuezov, is renowned as an encyclopedia of traditional

Kazakh culture and has been translated into all of the world's important languages. The 150th anniversary of the birth of Abay (1995) was proclaimed the "Year of Abay" by the United Nations Educational, Scientific and Cultural Organization (UNESCO) and was observed by the entire enlightened world. The name Abay has been given to boulevards, theaters, schools, institutes and universities. His poems are known and loved as immortal classics of Kazakhstan.

The legendary life of Zhambïl Zhabayev, which spanned almost a century, is known to every inhabitant of Kazakhstan. His uniqueness lies not only in his poetic works, but in the mission that history and fate placed upon him. Zhambïl was born on February 28, 1846, in Semirechye (Zhetysu, in Kazakh). Between 1870 and 1912, he was an invincible participant in "dueling" competitions (*aytïs*) among poets, 10 of which are ensconced in the treasury of Kazakh poetry. In 1919 Zhambïl was the winner of the first gathering of poets in Zhetisu, and in 1934 of the first republic-wide gathering of artistic masters of Kazakhstan. He participated four times in the festivals of Kazakh culture in Moscow, including the first in 1936. He was a master and performer of *dastans*, lyric-epic poems such as *A Thousand and One Nights*, *Shahname, Leyla and Mäzhnun*, *Qïz-Zhibek*, and *Edigey*. He was the author of the epic poems *Ötegen-batïr* and *Suranshi-batïr*. The life of Zhambïl coincided with the most tragic period of the Soviet dissolution and destruction of traditional nomadic culture and the forced transformation of oral culture into a written one. Zhambïl became a symbol of this period that destroyed Kazakh history. He was both its glory and its victim. As with the sesquicentennial of Abay, the 150th anniversary of the birth of Zhambïl was observed in 1996 as a national holiday and as an international celebration.

Each hero of Kazakh figurative art deserves individual attention, but this brief survey must suffice for now. What must be acknowledged is that the need inherent in Kazakh culture to know one's history found fertile ground in its figurative art. The desire and necessity to capture history on canvas and stone, to preserve its memory and make it the property of everyone, is still alive and well today. With the gaining of independence, Kazakh history itself is being resurrected. We witness not only the names of heroes returning, but their images as well. These include fighters for the independence of the Kazakh state during the time of the Dzungar invasions – Naurïzbay-batïr, Bögenbay-batïr, Qabanbay-batïr – as well as great khans such as Abïlay (1713-1781) and Kenesarï (1802-1847).

Modern figurative art is both mature and young at the same time. Masters of the late-20th and early-21st centuries are once again uncovering and embracing traditional values and are realizing their own creative discoveries in works that correspond to the spiritual and esthetic demands of their contemporaries. For contemporary artists, the entire millennia-long history of the Kazakh steppes, beginning with the prehistoric petroglyphs has once again become accessible, nativized and palpable. The Golden Warrior from the Issïq burial site has become their con-

temporary and is in many ways closer to them than the decrepit ideological idols of the 20th century. Pictures, drawings and sculptures cease to be copies of material reality and aspire to realize the cosmic worldview of the nomads. Through ideas derived from the images of the solar deities of the Tamghalï Valley mentioned earlier, contemporary artists are trying to restore not just Kazakh but nomadic

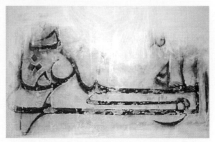

ARABIC CALLIGRAPHY AT 15TH-CENTURY ABDEL-AZIZ BABA MAUSOLEUM

civilization to their rightful place in history and esthetics.

Art is returning from the silence of museums to occupy its legitimate place among the lives of people as an integral part of the modern Kazakh city. Already this is not the canonical art of ornamentation created by the anonymous artists of past centuries, but a personal vision – an artist's own impression of the world as a contribution to the revival of ethnic culture. A number of contemporary artists are striving to revive traditional crafts like leather working, wood carving or working with metal or jewelry, such as D. Shoqparulï. Others, such as B. Zaubekova and S. Bul'trikov, are using the materials and techniques of traditional rug weaving or the preparation of felt rugs or reed mats to create unique artistic "canvases." They are using not just traditional materials or techniques, but even individual motifs of traditional art, though they are adapting them in unique

individual interpretations. The elements of ornamentation are being taken from their original applied settings and given an expression and passion that correspond to modern dynamics.

Inspired by the traditional folk crafts of southern Kazakhstan, masters such as Zhangir Umbetov and Amangul Ikhanova not only create new decorative objects based in tradition, but they have also created an innovative applied art called *küshkon*, which literally means "feeling-skin." Through their entire production process, from the preparation of the hide to its dyeing and cutting, these artists have shown their contemporaries the endless possibilities of various materials and found new degrees of plasticity and texture. They have enabled viewers to feel the unexpectedness and symbolism of their creations, relying on the most delicate of artistic sensitivities. The result is the creation of works that invite thought – concentrated attention that sparks an internal dialogue. This is the art of empathy, with an ability to take delight in nuances. It is an art that is particularly Kazakh. People who are skilled in the subtleties of cuisine that entice one to guess and identify which of its thousand different forms a favorite dish has taken find it natural to express a myriad of meanings through the same symbol or ornament and convey a spectrum of associations and meanings with a single word.

This art is akin to the Kazakh's ability to take delight in the tunes of songs called *küys* whose limitless variety unfolds through a quiet and loving contemplation of the music. In brief, Kazakh art is refined and aristocratic, and it offers pleasure and rewards that the rest of the world has yet to fully discover.

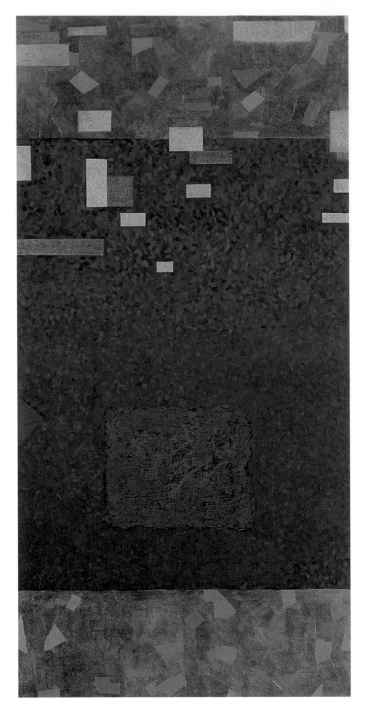

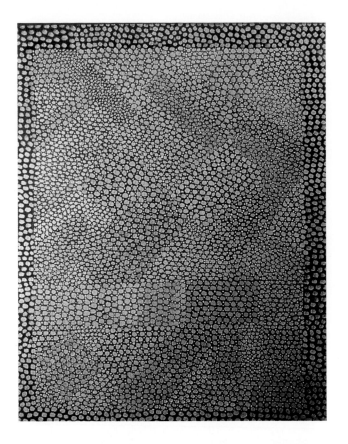

**TENGRI PICTOGRAPH**, 1995. GALYM MADANOV. OIL, SAND AND BRONZE ON CANVAS. 120 X 60 CENTIMETERS (47 X 23 INCHES). MOST GALLERY, ALMATY

**KUEZ-NUR** (INTERNAL LIGHT), 1997. KALIOLLA AKHMETZHAN. OIL ON CANVAS. PRIVATE COLLECTION.

**FIGHT**, 1989. ZHUMAKYN KAIRAMBAYEV. OIL ON CANVAS. THIS PAINTING ILLUSTRATES THE STRUGGLE BETWEEN WHITE AND BLACK AND GOOD AND EVIL. TENGRI UMAI GALLERY, ALMATY.

WHEN THE OPERA HOUSE IN ALMATY
WAS BEING RENOVATED IN 1997,
STUDENTS WERE INVITED TO DECORATE
THE CONSTRUCTION WALL AROUND
THE BUILDING. THIS PAINTING ON ONE
OF THE PLYWOOD PANELS IS BY ALEX
LUOVICH.

ZHARAPAZAN, 1996. TIMUR ASYLBEKOV.
OIL ON CANVAS. THIS PAINTING DEPICTS
THE SPRING FESTIVAL OF NAURÏZ THAT
CELEBRATES THE VENERATION OF LIFE
AND NATURE, THE END OF DARKNESS
AND THE BEGINNING OF LIGHT. PEOPLE
ARE REQUIRED TO END THEIR DISPUTES
AND CULTIVATE PEACE FOR THE NEW
YEAR. MOST GALLERY, ALMATY.

OCTOBER REVOLUTION, 1988.
VLADIMIR LUKIN.
THE PAINTING TELLS THE STORY
OF THE BOLSHEVIKS' ARRIVAL IN
KAZAKHSTAN.
PRIVATE COLLECTION.

MANGHYSTAU, 1997. AMANGUL
IKHANOVA AND ZHANGIR UMBETOV.
LEATHER, MOSAIC, STAMPING AND
RELIEF. THE ARTISTS DEVELOPED A
TECHNIQUE, CALLED **KÜSHKON**,
USING DYED LEATHER IN A MOSAIC
THAT IS EMBOSSED AND WORKED IN
RELIEF. THEY EXPLOIT THE AMBIGUITY
OF THIS TECHNIQUE TO EXPLORE
METAPHYSICAL IDEAS. THIS IMAGE
MERGES LIGHT AND COLOR, ILLOGICAL
FORMS AND SUN GODS TO EXPRESS
THE ARTISTS' IDEAS ABOUT THE ORIGIN
OF THE WORLD.

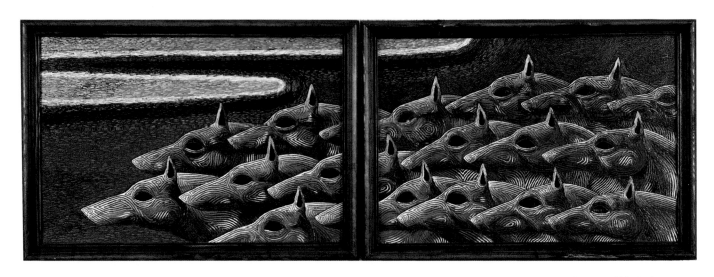

THE PACK, 1998. SHAMIL
M. GULIEV. OIL ON CANVAS.
DIPTYCH, 50 X 75 CENTIMETERS
(20 X 29 INCHES). THIS
PAINTING ILLUSTRATES THAT
IF ALL THE TURKIC TRIBES
JOINED TOGETHER THEY
WOULD BE STRONG LIKE A
WOLF PACK.
MOST GALLERY, ALMATY.

SACRIFICE, 1991. ASKAR
ESDAULETOV. OIL ON
CANVAS.
TENGRI UMAI GALLERY, ALMATY.

YURI SUPPES PAINTS A MURAL IN THE DOME OF ZENKOV CATHEDRAL, BUILT BETWEEN 1904 AND 1907, IN PANFILOV PARK IN ALMATY. THE CHURCH'S FORMAL NAME IS SVYATO-VOZNESENSKY CATHEDRAL.

THE INTERIOR OF ZENKOV CATHEDRAL REMAINED UNPAINTED FROM THE TIME IT WAS COMPLETED IN 1907 UNTIL 1997.
ARTIST VLADIMIR LUKIN HAS CHOSEN BRIGHT YELLOWS AND BLUES TO REFLECT THAT THIS IS A TIME OF HOPE
FOR THE FUTURE OF KAZAKHSTAN AND AS AN EXPRESSION OF FAITH.

THE FIGURE ABOVE DEPICTS TOMYRIS, QUEEN OF THE MASSAGETAES, A TRIBE THAT WAS PART OF THE SCYTHIAN FEDERATION IN THE 6TH CENTURY B.C. HER STORY IS ONE OF THE GREAT TALES IN KAZAKH EPIC HISTORY: CYRUS, THE HANDSOME KING OF PERSIA, INVADED WHAT IS NOW SOUTHERN KAZAKHSTAN IN 529 B.C. HE TRIED TO WOO TOMYRIS, BUT SHE REBUFFED HIM. AN AIDE TOLD HIM, "IT IS A SHAME THAT CYRUS SHOULD YIELD TO A WOMAN." THUS INCITED, CYRUS SET A TRAP. HE SENT PART OF HIS ARMY OUT, CARRYING A FEAST. TOMYRIS SENT HER SON, SPARGAPISES, A GENERAL, TO TURN THE PERSIANS BACK. AFTER DEFEATING THEM, SPARGAPISES AND HIS TROOPS SAT DOWN TO THE FOOD AND STRONG WINE. THEN, WHILE THEY SLEPT, CYRUS TOOK SPARGAPISES CAPTIVE. WHEN TOMYRIS LEARNED THIS, SHE SENT A HERALD TO CYRUS SAYING, "YOU HAVE OVERPOWERED MY SON BY TRICKERY, NOT BY STRENGTH. FREE HIM AND LEAVE MY COUNTRY AT ONCE. IF YOU DO NOT, FOR ALL YOUR BLOOD LUST, I WILL GIVE YOU YOUR FILL OF IT." THE PERSIANS FREED HIM, BUT SPARGAPISES TOOK HIS OWN LIFE IN SHAME. WHEN TOMYRIS HEARD, SHE GATHERED HER FORCES. HERODOTUS RECORDS THAT CYRUS AND MOST OF THE PERSIAN ARMY DIED IN THE CATACLYSMIC BATTLE THAT FOLLOWED. TOMYRIS SOUGHT OUT HIS CORPSE, FILLED A SKIN WITH HUMAN BLOOD, AND PLACED CYRUS'S HEAD IN IT. "I AM THE CONQUEROR," SHE SAID, "BUT YOU HAVE DESTROYED ME ALL THE SAME BY ROBBING ME OF MY SON. NOW I GIVE YOU YOUR FILL OF BLOOD, JUST AS I THREATENED."

CRADLE OF CENTURIES ETHNOLOGY MUSEUM, ALMATY.

SCULPTORS PERNEGUL OMAROVA AND ZHANNUR ALIMBAYEV, HER HUSBAND, CREATE EXQUISITE DOLLS THAT DEPICT FIGURES IN KAZAKH HISTORY TO TEACH CHILDREN ABOUT THEIR HERITAGE. THE FIGURE RECEIVING FINISHING TOUCHES TO ITS HELMET AT TOP IS OF THE 18TH-CENTURY STEPPE KNIGHT, QABANBAY-BATÏR. BELOW IS THE FIGURE OF ASAN QAYGHI, THE ACCLAIMED 15TH-CENTURY AQÏN, POET AND MUSICIAN. HE WAS KNOWN AS THE "ETERNAL TRAVELER" WHO SEARCHED FOR A PARADISE ON EARTH AND LEARNED THAT IT COULD BE FOUND IN HIS OWN LAND. IN 1999, THE CRADLE OF CENTURIES ETHNOLOGY MUSEUM OPENED IN ALMATY TO HOUSE THEIR COLLECTION.

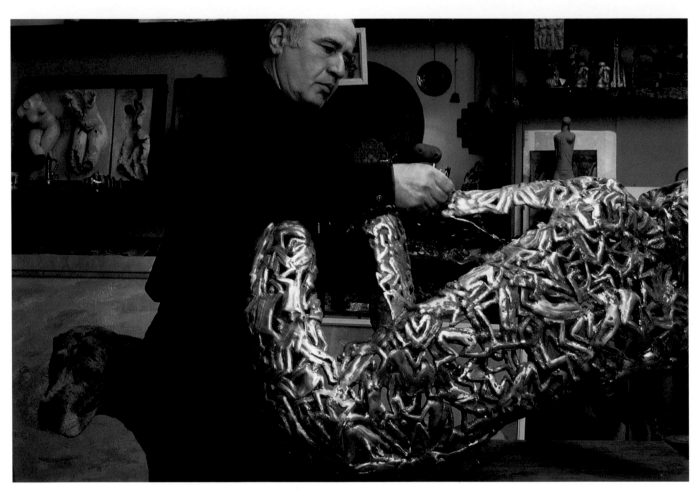

"RENOIR, A BEAUTIFUL, GENTLE GREAT DANE, MET US AT THE GATE OF THE ALMATY STUDIO SHARED BY HUSBAND AND WIFE SCULP-TORS VAGIF RAHMANOV AND MARINA RESHETNIKOVA. VAGIF'S WORKS CAN BE FOUND IN MUSEUMS AND PRIVATE COLLECTIONS AROUND THE WORLD. HERE HE REPAIRS A 1995 BRONZE CALLED DANTE. RENOIR, THE DOG, PEERS OUT TO APPRAISE ME FROM BEHIND THE SCULPTOR. ON THE OPPOSITE PAGE, MARINA PREPARES A WAX MODEL OF A NEW PIECE, CALLED MEDUSA." – W.E.

UMAY (MOTHER GODDESS). 1995. MARINA RESHETNIKOVA. SCULPTURE IN BRONZE.

ZHANNUR ALIMBAYEV AND HIS WIFE, PERNEGUL OMAROVA, WERE TRAINED AS SCULPTORS AT THE PRESTIGIOUS ART ACADEMY OF I. REPIN IN ST. PETERSBURG. THEIR COLLABORATIVE CREATIONS OF HISTORICAL KAZAKH FIGURES ARE WIDELY SOUGHT BY INTERNATIONAL COLLECTORS. HERE ZHANNUR PUTS THE FINISHING TOUCHES ON A MINIATURE FIGURE. HE IS CURRENTLY WORKING ON A SET OF NETSUKE.

ETERNITY, 1998. M. KOZHAMKULOV. WOOL. WOVEN IN SHYMKENT, SOUTHERN KAZAKHSTAN. THIS TAPESTRY REFLECTS THE CONTINUATION OF LIFE THROUGH THE FAMILY AND INCLUDES MANY TRADITIONAL MOTIFS. CENTRAL EXHIBIT HALL, ALMATY.

AL FARABI 1990S. AYSBEK AKHMETOV. SCULPTURE IN **SHAMOT** (A MIXTURE OF CLAY AND GROUND CHINA). AL FARABI WAS AN ISLAMIC PHILOSOPHER AND RENOWNED MUSICAL THEORIST WHO WROTE AN ENCYCLOPEDIC WORK RECONCILING ARISTOTLE AND ISLAM. HE WAS ALSO A SUFI MYSTIC. HE WAS BORN IN OTRAR IN SOUTHERN KAZAKHSTAN ABOUT 870 A.D.

JUGGLER OF HUMAN SOULS, 1997. AIZHAN BEKKULOVA. PAPER GRAPHIC. PRIVATE COLLECTION.

THIS CARVED WOODEN DOOR IS ON THE ENTRANCE TO A TRADING HOUSE ON THE ROUTE OF THE OLD SILK ROAD.
IT DATES TO THE LATE 19TH CENTURY.

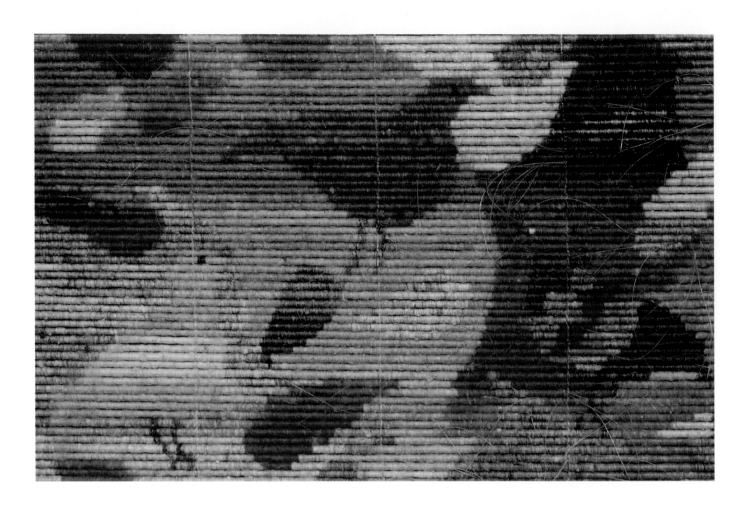

BIRDS OF HAPPINESS, 1998. RAIGUL AKHMETZHANOVA. WOOL-WRAPPED REEDS. DECORATIVE CHI. PRIVATE COLLECTION.

SAGYM (MIRAGE), 1994. B. TURGENBAYEV. OIL ON CANVAS. TENGRI UMAI GALLERY, ALMATY.

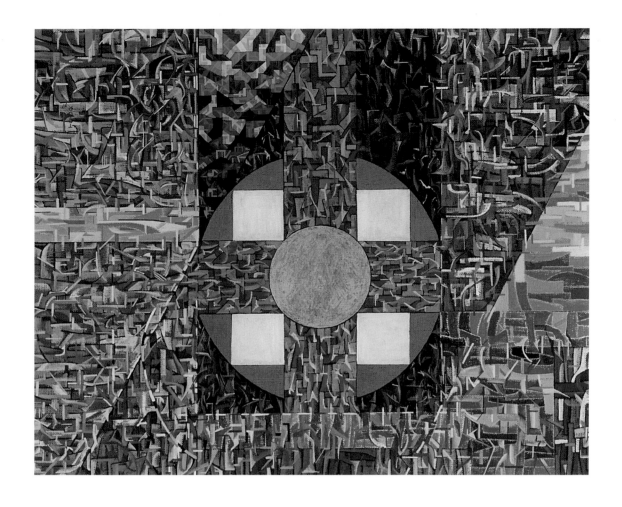

BIRTH OF THE EARTH, 1997. ALEXANDER OSIPOV. OIL ON CANVAS. 69 X 89 CENTIMETERS (27 X 35 INCHES). MOST GALLERY, ALMATY.

KORAN, 18TH CENTURY. GABDUR-RASUL. 35 X 53 CENTIMETERS (14 X 21 INCHES), 521 PAGES. THIS IS A COVER FOR AN ILLUMINATED MANUSCRIPT WITH ELABORATE FLORAL AND GOLD-PAINTED CALF-LEATHER BINDING.
RARE BOOK SECTION, NATIONAL LIBRARY OF KAZAKHSTAN, ALMATY.

THE WOLF IS A TOTEMIC ANIMAL IN KAZAKHSTAN, AND THE WOLF'S HEAD SHOWN HERE IS A REPRODUCTION OF A DECORATION ATOP A STANDARD FOUND IN THE NORTH OF KAZAKHSTAN THAT IS NOW IN THE HERMITAGE MUSEUM IN ST. PETERSBURG. IT WAS MADE BY KRYM ALTYNBEKOV OF GILDED COPPER AND SILVER. WOLF BANNERS OR STANDARDS LIKE THIS ONE WERE OFTEN CARRIED INTO BATTLE BY WARRIORS. A MEMBRANE INSIDE THE WOLF'S MOUTH MADE A PIERCING SOUND WHEN THE STANDARD WAS HELD ALOFT WHILE GALLOPING.

KRYM ALTYNBEKOV, ARTIST AND GOLDSMITH, WORKS ON A NEW PIECE IN HIS ALMATY STUDIO. HE IS THE LEADING RESTORATION ARTIST IN THE COUNTRY AND HAS CREATED WIDELY EXHIBITED REPRODUCTIONS OF THE GOLDEN WARRIOR. ANOTHER EXAMPLE OF HIS WORK IS ON THE FACING PAGE.

"IT TOOK KAINEKE ZARYKPAI-KYZY KANAPYANOVA TWO YEARS TO CREATE THIS EMBROIDERED-FELT TUSKIIZ. SHE MADE IT AS A WEDDING GIFT FOR HER SON, NURGAZY, IN 1973. WHEN I TOLD HER SHE WAS A MASTER LIKE THE ARTISTS IN JAPAN CALLED 'NATIONAL TREASURES,' SHE SAID, 'THANK YOU.' AFTER A PAUSE SHE ASKED, 'WILL YOU PUT THAT IN YOUR BOOK?'"
– W.E.

THIS ARCHITECTURAL MODEL IS ONE OF THE PROPOSALS FOR THE NEW GOVERNMENT CENTER IN ASTANA, WHICH BECAME KAZAKHSTAN'S CAPITAL IN 1998. THE BUILDING CONCEPT WAS DESIGNED AND DEVELOPED BY ARCHITECT BEK IBRAYEV AND HIS STAFF. ITS COMPOSITION IS BASED ON PRINCIPLES OF ORGANIZED SPACE USED IN ANCIENT TURKIC AND HUNNISH HEADQUARTERS. THE "SENIOR YURT," WHERE DECISIONS THAT AFFECT THE WHOLE COUNTRY ARE MADE, IS PLACED IN THE CENTER. AS IN ANCIENT TIMES, THE MAIN AXES OF THE PROPOSED BUILDING ARE STRICTLY ORIENTED ON A NORTH-SOUTH, EAST-WEST BASIS TO SECURE THE PATRONAGE OF THE HIGHER POWERS AND BRING WELL-BEING AND GOOD FORTUNE TO THE COUNTRY AND ITS LEADERS.

THIS BEAUTIFULLY DETAILED AND ILLUMINATED MANUSCRIPT IN ARABIC IS CALLED **DIVANI** (A COLLECTION OF SONGS). THE WORKS OF ALISHER NAVOYII (1441-1501) WERE WELL KNOWN IN PARTS OF CENTRAL ASIA AND THE MIDDLE EAST IN THE 15TH CENTURY. THIS 844-PAGE VOLUME WAS CREATED IN 1649. RARE BOOK SECTION, NATIONAL LIBRARY OF KAZAKHSTAN, ALMATY.

"SHAMIL M. GULIEV PAINTS FROM HIS SUBCONSCIOUS AND EMPLOYS LAYERS OF SYMBOLIC MEANINGS IN HIS CREATIONS. FOR THIS PHOTOGRAPH, I FITTED FOUR OF HIS CANVASES TOGETHER AND THUS WAS ABLE TO PLACE HIM INSIDE HIS DREAM WORLD." – W.E.

## POETRY AND PERFORMING ARTS: EXPRESSIONS OF THE SOUL

If you were to ask in what form the soul of the Kazakh people is best expressed, I would not hesitate to respond that it is best expressed in traditional Kazakh folk music. All aspects of Kazakh life are permeated with music; it infuses the entire universe of our culture. Music is heard on holidays and at gatherings, in ceremonies and rituals, at feasts and in daily life. Even the musical instruments are an acoustical embodiment of the traditional beliefs of the Kazakh people: the universal "Three Worlds" of the Upper, Middle, and Lower. These levels are represented first in the bowed string instrument called the *qïl qobïz*. Kazakh shamans

17TH-CENTURY QÏL QOBÏZ

known as *baqsï* developed this instrument and in its construction preserved the idea of creating sound from the friction of two hunting bows. The *qobïz* (pronounced ko-bis) is one of the world's oldest musical instruments. It is considered the ancestor of European string instruments played with a bow, including the violin.

Perhaps the greatest *qobïzshï*, or "*qobïz* composer/performer," was Ïqïlas Dükenulï (1843-1916), whose instrumental songs came to form the basis of the modern repertoire. The deep, vibrating, lower-register sounds of the *qobïz*, so rich in overtones, personifies the murmuring and rumbling of the Lower World, just as its upper register can express the dazzling, silvery radiance of the Upper World. A parallel to this symbolic range can be found in the reed wind instrument of the shepherds and pastoralists known as the *sïbïzghï*, whose low basic note or drone (the sound of the Lower World) and whistling melody (the sound of the Upper World) remind one of the magical throat singing of the Tuvans of southern Siberia. The *sïbïzghï* is a long, open flute played by men and corresponds to the *shan qobïz*, a so-called "Jew's harp," played by women, which also combines a basic tone (drone) with a melody. In the center of all this is the two-stringed, plucked instrument known as the *dombïra*, the instrument of the Middle World (the World of Human Beings). The *dombïra* – often pronounced and spelled "dombra" – is the inseparable companion of the nomad: a convivial, spiritual consort. Just as the Indian *tamboura* carries all the ragas within it, the *dombïra* figuratively contains not only a range of

DOMBÏRA, ALSO CALLED DOMBRA

musical information, but a range of ethnic information as well.

Poets of the past and present have dedicated hundreds of songs and poems to the *dombïra*. Its origins and history are layered with myths and legends. The *dombïra*, decorated with the feathers of an eagle or an owl, can be seen in the most honored place in the yurt or in a modern urban apartment. With a velvet voice, pulsating and warm, that creates the sensation of a boundless space, it is comparable in expressiveness and range to the human voice. The *dombïra* is used to accompany songs, and also to perform solo instrumental melodies known as *küys*. Some people believe that this name comes from the word *küy*, which refers to a "condition, state or mood." For it is in these *küy* songs that the subtle gradations of range and the full esthetic attractiveness and philosophical power of the art of the Kazakhs is best displayed.

Over the centuries, various styles of *dombïra* music developed across the vast territory of Kazakhstan. *Tökpe* – picking the strings with the fingers or nails to produce music in streams or bursts to accompany epic songs – was refined in the west. *Shertpe* – strumming with the fingers to produce music in a more lyrical sound – came from the east. Within these two major styles there are hundreds of compositional schools with their own local features.

Performances of *küy* songs are accompanied by narrative legends about the composer, the history and circumstances of its composition, and about its contents. This prepares the listener for the harmonies that are key to understanding the *küy* and to evoking the corresponding associations. Thus the *küyshis* – the professional folk musicians who perform this music – preserve for us not only the names but also the creations of composers from the distant or recent past, carefully passing on their repertoire from master to apprentice.

Among these composers are the legendary Qorqït (8th century), Ketbugha (9th century), Qaztughan (15th century), Bayzhigit (17th century) and Khan Abïlay (18th century).

The music of three great *küyshis* of the 19th century who were all alive at the same time – Tattimbet (1815-1862), Dauletkerey (1820-1887), and Qurmanghazï (1818-1889) – are as different from one another as the music of Haydn, Mozart and Beethoven, three classical Western composers from the same period. A comparison of Kazakh *küys* with the symphonic music of Europe is not such a wild jump artistically, according to several European experts. French writer and musicologist Romain Rolland and Russian composer and academician Boris Asafev, for example, posit that *küys* are equally intricate and highly developed in their own right.

For the nomads, the endless steppe framed by snow-capped mountains was the stage for all art, but particularly for the wordplay beloved by Kazakhs. This Art of the Word – an epithet for clever, flowery speech loaded with metaphors, proverbs, sayings and the art of allegory – struck travelers to the region as brilliant. Belief in the magical power of words – which Kazakhs compare to an arrow, a lance, a blade or lightning – demanded great attention to pronunciation, caution and responsibility in their use. Words can soothe and heal, but they can also wound and cripple. Even the name given to a person at birth somehow affects the course of his or her future life. Such Kazakh names as Azat (Free), Aqzhan (Honest), Zhantuar (Life Giver), Zhaqsïlïq (Goodness), Nurlan (Shining),

Tangïrbergen (God-given), Quan (Happy), Baqit (Happiness), or Säule (Shining), all speak for themselves. Each word, forged in the hearth of oral poetry, gives birth to a web of associations in life and in art

The Kazakh tradition of oral history preserves and transmits from generation to generation stories about the debates of great judges and philosophers. Their witty and brilliant ripostes and wise jurisprudence enter into proverbs that are used to resolve disputes and difficult entanglements. The origins, status, wisdom and talent of the interlocutor are still judged by the style of his speech. This art was sharpened over the centuries within the framework of ritual language. Using this framework, one masters various styles and formulas of communication depending upon one's age, social status and specific situation.

The zenith of such communication is the musical-poetic contest known as the *aytïs* – verbal dueling between singers, called *aqïn*, before a large and knowledgeable audience. The language forms in an *aytïs* are so complex, and the nuances and associations so arcane, that a meaningful translation to another language is virtually impossible.

There is a tremendous variety of *aytïs* within Kazakh poetic culture: *qïz ben zhigit aytïsï*, for example, is a verbal duel between a girl and boy; *din aytïsï* is a verbal duel about religion; *zhumbaq aytïsï*, a verbal duel with riddles; *aqïndar aytïsï*, a verbal duel between bards;

and so on. There were even verbal duels between bards on narrow themes – to test the contestants' geographic knowledge, for example. Weddings were scenes of mass competitive song improvisations. Instrumental music competitions, called *tartïs*, were also popular. Each kind of *aytïs* or *tartïs* was an event with great social significance.

Groups of itinerant singers and bards (*aqïns*) also existed. Along with musicians, these groups traditionally included a humorist-wit, a smith-jeweler and a strongman-wrestler. In the make-up of such "brigades," it was as though the implied poetic metaphors had been

FIGURE OF QORQÏT ATA, CREATOR OF THE **QOBÏZ**

personified – the "forging" of a word, a *triumphant* word, a *muscular* word, and a *striking* or *well-aimed* word. The image and

its embodiment traveled together, the word being sharpened simultaneously as an idea and as a visible action.

The activities of the *aqïn*, or bard, can be compared with the ancient Greek *aed* who represented his tribe in poetic song competitions. The Kazakh word *ayt-ïs* literally means "to speak together" and refers to a verbal duel, usually a dialogical competition between two or more poets or poet-singers. Such *aytïs* competitions are so loved by Kazakhs and so intense that they can last from morning until midnight – and sometimes even until dawn. Poetry competitions originated on social holidays and feasts, and were eagerly anticipated opportunities for people to test their verbal wit and mettle. According to custom the loser must recite the entire competition from memory, with all of its dialogues and rejoinders. Folklore has preserved a classic example of such an *aytïs* from the end of the 19th century: "Birzhan-Sara" records the duel between Sara Tastanbekqïzï, a brilliant young poetess-*aqïn*, who lost to the noted poet-*aqïn* Birzhan-sal Qozhaghululï. (It is worth noting that in poetic duels women and men have equal standing and compete on equal footing.)

A first-rate *aytïs* contains all the elements of good theater – the suspense of a game; the circle of experienced, knowledgeable spectators; and the highest level of masterful performances. Thus in the early 1930s, when dramatic and later operatic theaters began to become well organized, the

folk performing arts tradition was not diminished but enhanced and soon became a beloved form of modern Kazakh art.

The first Kazakh opera, *Qïz-Zhibek* debuted in 1936 at the first ten-day Festival of the Arts of Kazakhstan in Moscow. The heroes of this opera are as well known to every Kazakh as Romeo and Juliet are to any European. Composer Yevgenii Brusilovskii created his opera on an *epic* subject, but used as a basis *lyrical* songs that were recorded from folk singers and musicians, who would actually perform in the opera. That first production of the opera at the 1936 festival was strung with the best pearls of lyrical folk music; the costumes shone with perfection and were striking for their ethnographic accuracy; and the creators and the performers were so inspired that it remains a classic today. It was the first time that operatic arias were sung on an equal basis with folk songs, and accounts of those first performances are memories cherished by the older generation of Kazakhs.

With the birth of opera, the star of Kulyash Bayseitova, the silvery-voiced natural coloratura soprano, also rose. My mother remembers to this day the roles Kulyash Bayseitova sang, ranging from the lead in *Qïz-Zhibek* to Cio-Cio-San in Puccini's *Madama Butterfly*. My mother's recollections say more to me about the cultural life of Kazakhstan in the 1940s and 1950s than many scholarly volumes about the subject. During the time of the Great

Patriotic War, students of the newly established Women's Pedagogical Institute, half-starved and weakened, would walk along the dusty streets to the Opera Theater carrying cloth shoes they had whitened with chalk. They would wash up in the clear water of the irrigation ditches, pretty themselves up, put on their shoes, and then enter the auditorium to encounter their beloved songs, heroes and performers. They knew the performers, idolized them and imitated them. During the most difficult times the theater gave people the strength to live, to hope and to fight. They awaited each new operatic or theatrical production impatiently, rushed to the premiere, memorized the poetic texts of the libretto and the stage directions, and learned the songs by heart to sing them at home.

The 1944 opera *Abay*, mentioned in Chapter 5, was devoted to the life of the great poet and thinker Abay Qunanbay. It, too, has become a beloved classic, and productions of it can still be seen today. The gradual development of the young art of opera in Kazakhstan is perhaps best represented by the 1947 opera *Birzhan and Sara* by Muqan Tölebaev, who based it on the *aytïs* mentioned earlier in this chapter. Tölebaev's work was devoted to the poetic competitions and loves of notable bards. This was already a departure from a *citational* opera based on the literal use of folk melodies. Much of

Tölebaev's own music followed the emerging form of the new national operatic style.

During those same years, the Kazakh epic also found its own realization on the stage as a genre of dramatic performance. The gala opening of the Kazakh National Theater took place in 1926. The talented director and playwright Zhumat Shanin worked there. Plays named after epic heroes such as *Qaraqïpshaq Qoblandï*, *Er-Targhïn*, *Beket*, and *Arqalïq* that were produced in the 1920s through the 1940s still form a part of the repertoire of Kazakh theater. Mukhtar Äuezov created the popular play *Ayman-Sholpan* in 1934 for the Kazakh State Musical-Dramatic Theater. The Zhambïl Zhabayev Kazakh State Philharmonium was established in 1935. Its composition included the Qurmanghazï Orchestra of Folk Instruments, a Kazakh chorus, a dance ensemble, and a large group of soloists singing folk songs and performing on musical instruments.

National folk dances already occupied an important place in the very first theatrical and operatic productions. If lyrical folk singing was transplanted to the stage practically in its entirety – with only some new words and a new arrangement – dance demanded a serious rethinking. Kazakh folk dances were closely intertwined with rituals such as the shamans' ceremony for healing the sick or the collective Sufi *zikr*, a chant used by Muslim mystics to achieve religious ecstasy. Dance was also an integral part of

wedding games and sports competitions. Ritual poses, games and activities taken from folk culture, along with the symbolism of gestures and ornaments, were adapted to the stage in such folk dances as *Orteke* (The Mountain Goat in a Trap), *Qoyan-Bürkit* (The Hare and the Eagle), and *Örmekbi* (The Weaving Dance). Shara Zhienbaeva was the greatest Kazakh dancer of this period who performed not just Kazakh dances, but dance forms from around the world.

Another unique development in the cultural life of Kazakhstan began in the 1960s. The Young Ballet of Kazakhstan was founded by Bulat Ayukhanov who became its permanent leader. This troupe combined the achievements of classical and folk dance and established the National Ballet of Kazakhstan that absorbed and assimilated within itself a wealth of 20th-century culture.

The heroes who take the stage in all these operas, ballets and dramas were gestated during the many-centuries-long epic tradition. The epic songs, exhortations and legends live on today in these new and beloved forms of professional folk creativity. This tradition of the epic in the oral literature is where Kazakhs have always expressed their history and philosophy. In their totality, the epic genres, both large and small, gather and articulate the traditional moral code that affirms the entire value system that binds the ethnic group together. Functionally, the dominant characteristic of the epic tradition is its openly didactic quality – a way of addressing one's own people in a sermonizing manner. Historically, the epic tale was literally a road map for regulating social relations, directing the private life into a channel of eternity and concentrating in the present moment all that is past and yet to come. The very life of the nomad required a command of knowledge about the past in order to survive in the present and thrive in the future. The epic tale was the only mechanism versatile enough to transmit the historical experience of the Kazakhs across the centuries.

For epic performance to function at its optimum level, it is essential to have an audience that was brought up in the traditional value system. The epic clearly and expressly addresses the theater audience presupposing that it will understand all of the nuances and actively participate. The audience acts as a collective censor and engages in a collective dialogue with the teller of the epic tale. Through all of this, the "epic audience" absorbs, embodies and preserves the experience of Kazakh history, and thus promotes new tellers of the tales from within its ranks. In the difficult wartime and postwar periods, the natural rhythms of Kazakh life and tradition were destroyed; and it was the epic audience that preserved the epic tradition and led to its rebirth in what was then the Qïzïlorda Oblast,

where it has flourished for the past few decades.

The epic singers who embody this collective memory had great social status and were called – and are still known to this day – as *zhïraus*. Traditionally, the *zhïraus* were counselors to the khan, the preservers of epic history and successors to the shamans. Their work helped to bind and

KENEN AZERBAEV, FAMOUS SINGER AND TRADITIONAL COMPOSER (1884 - 1976)

unify the generations to form an ethnic consciousness. The epic singer sees his performance not as "singing songs," but as a lofty mission to which he has a calling. In the act of making music, the epic singer gives voice to the entire epic world and thereby unites the singular, finite world of human beings with the totality and infiniteness of the folk consciousness. During his performance the personality of the epic singer becomes a doorway – a point of transit that links the *present*, the heroic *past* and the *future*. As the *zhïraus* themselves attest, the life of a

human spirit is measured by the sum total of its moments in communion with the epic singing. The remaining time – the time between epic perform-ances – are merely transitory moments of existence nurtured by the memory of the great epic revelations.

Even today the Kazakh people continue to believe that the talents of the epic singers are "magical," based not only on their remarkable ability to memorize prodigious quantities of text, but on the power and emotional influence of their manner of singing. In discussions with *zhïraus*, I have heard on more than one occasion expressions such as *arqasï bar*, which means "there is the sensation of a spirit-protector behind him," or *arqasï qozïp ketti*, meaning "his back ignited," which indicates that he is in a state of ecstasy. The information that the *zhïrau* conveys to his listeners consists not only of a poetic text. As with any great orator, the *zhïrau* uses all the means available to him to influence his audience. This is a kind of speech that is dramatically intense and richly expressive, and is oratorical by its very nature.

By the 1850s and until the early part of the 20th century, Kazakh folk-professional lyric music flourished. The types of performers of lyric songs – *änshi*, *sal* and *seri*, meaning "the singer," the "dandy," and the "golden-tongued one"– can be compared with the knight-courtesan tradition of Western European troubadours whose art also sang of beauty and harmony. Aleksandr Zataevich, the great collector of the oral tradition of Kazakh music, called this phenomenon "Kazakh troubadourism." These professional performers of epic lyric song were distinguished by their refined dress and the extravagance of their behavior – they were the favorites, the "spoiled children" of the people. The clearest forms of Kazakh

QURMANGHAZÏ, GREAT KÜYSHI (FOLK MUSICIAN)

professional lyric song belong to the Central Kazakhstan region of Sarïarqa (Golden Steppe), where the Arqa School produced dozens of famous singers during the second half of the 19th century and the beginning of the 20th. One of these, Amre Qashaubayulï, became widely known outside Kazakhstan when he appeared to great acclaim at two international art expositions. The first was

in Paris in 1925, where he received second prize, and the second in Frankfurt am Main in 1927. His voice is preserved on a vinyl record produced in the 1970s from cylinder rolls recorded in Moscow in the 1920s. The 20th-century successors to the great singer-composer tradition – Manarbek Erzhanov, Zhusupbek Elebekov, Zhanïbek Qarmenov – made it possible to preserve the national treasure of Kazakh lyric song and to savor it in modern life.

The 1960s and 1970s were a turning point in Kazakh musical culture. During this period there was rebirth of interest in traditional culture, its history and its originality. This interest sparked a deeper study of the oral musical tradition. One result was the establishment in 1981 of Otrar Sazï, an orchestra of folk instruments led by the composer and *dombïra* player Nurgis Tlendiev. It includes a large number of unique non-European ethnic instruments such as the *sïbïzghï* (reed flute), the *saz-sïrnay* (clay flute), the *sherter* (a three-stringed instrument played by plucking) and other instruments. This type of collective performance became a model for a large number of amateur ensembles as well.

The 1990s saw the phenomenon of young rock and pop music groups becoming interested in traditional music. Using the style and techniques of rock and pop bands to play music based on the Kazakh oral tradition, the resulting hybrid broke new ground. Kazakhstan

took center court by staging the international Aziya Dausï or "Voice of Asia" Festival, which was intended to spotlight and promote ethnic-inspired rock and pop music from all over the Asian continent. The clearest Kazakh phenomenon in this genre was the popular group Roksonakï, which won first prize in the Festival. Ancient Kazakh songs and epic exhortations resounded again as interpreted and translated into the sounds and music of contemporary youth.

Thus the great tradition of expression of the national spirit through music, words and dance seems timeless. Throughout the centuries, it remained intact. What once seemed broken was only a pause before it sent out new shoots like the Tree of Life and renewed almost every aspect of the national culture. Today, the Kazakh people are finding how the ancient truths reflect the spiritual needs of the present.

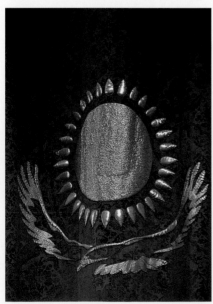

EMBROIDERED SYMBOL OF THE REPUBLIC OF KAZAKHSTAN

A WELL-USED CONDUCTOR'S SCORE SITS ON THE PODIUM FOLLOWING A PERFORMANCE
AT THE PALACE OF THE REPUBLIC IN ALMATY.

A FIRST-RATE **AYTÏS**, A PERFORMANCE COMPETITION BETWEEN
SINGERS/POETS KNOWN AS **AQÏNS**, CONTAINS THE ESSENCE OF
THEATER – THE ELEMENT OF A GAME, THE CIRCLE OF EXPERIENCED,
KNOWLEDGEABLE SPECTATORS AND THE HIGHEST LEVEL OF MASTERY
BY THE PERFORMERS. THE **AYTÏS** UNDERWAY HERE IS THE ANNUAL
COMPETITION IN ALMATY HELD AT THE PALACE OF THE REPUBLIC.

THE CREATIVE DISCOVERY CONCERT SHOWCASES WINNERS OF
INTERNATIONAL MUSIC COMPETITIONS. HERE A PERFORMER WEARING
A TRADITIONAL EMBROIDERED VELVET **SHAPAN** (COAT) AND **AIYRKALPAK**
(HAT) PLAYS THE **DOMBÏRA** AT CENTRAL CONCERT HALL IN ALMATY.

KAZAKHS LOVE MUSIC OF ALL KINDS AND FILL THE CONCERT HALLS TO HEAR BOTH TRADITIONAL AND WESTERN MUSIC,
BELOVED KAZAKH ARTISTS, CONSERVATORY STUDENTS MAKING THEIR DEBUTS OR INTERNATIONAL GUEST ARTISTS.
HERE AN ALMATY AUDIENCE ENJOYS A PERFORMANCE AT THE CENTRAL CONCERT HALL.

A MODERN-DANCE PERFORMANCE WAS PRESENTED BY THE BALLET SCHOOL OF KAMILLA ISMAILOVA IN SEMEY
IN EASTERN KAZAKHSTAN AS PART OF THE ÄUEZOV JUBILEE CELEBRATION IN 1997.

A DANCER FROM THE YOUNG BALLET OF ALMATY PERFORMS AN ORIGINAL WORK, CHOREOGRAPHED
BY BULAT AYUKHANOV BASED ON TRADITIONAL KAZAKH DANCE, AT THE PALACE OF THE REPUBLIC.

BULAT AYUKHANOV IS THE
FOUNDER AND ARTISTIC
DIRECTOR OF THE YOUNG
BALLET OF ALMATY. HE
BEGAN IT IN 1966 AS A
CHAMBER BALLET. TODAY
THEIR ECLECTIC PROGRAMS
INCLUDE ORIGINAL
WORKS, BALLETS BASED ON
TRADITIONAL KAZAKH
DANCE AND MUSIC, AND
CLASSICAL BALLETS. HERE HE
WRAPS HIS LEGS IN
PREPARATION FOR A
REHEARSAL.

A WEEK OF PERFORMANCES
AND WORKSHOPS CALLED
"KAZAKHSTANIS – WORLD
BALLET STARS," WAS RECENTLY
PRODUCED IN ALMATY TO
INSPIRE YOUNG KAZAKH
DANCERS. THE TEACHERS
AND SOLOISTS WERE EXCEP-
TIONAL KAZAKH DANCERS
FROM BALLET COMPANIES
IN GERMANY, RUSSIA,
SLOVENIA, THE UNITED
STATES, AND KAZAKHSTAN.
THE PHOTO WAS TAKEN AT
A PERFORMANCE OF **SWAN
LAKE** AT THE PALACE OF
THE REPUBLIC.

THE CORPS DE BALLET FOR "KAZAKHSTANIS – WORLD BALLET STARS" INCLUDED DANCERS FROM THE ABAY THEATER OF OPERA AND BALLET AND SELEZNEV'S SCHOOL OF BALLET.

A DANCER WITH THE YOUNG BALLET OF ALMATY RESTS DURING REHEARSALS FOR AN ORIGINAL BALLET, **EDITH PIAF**, BASED ON THE FRENCH SINGER'S LIFE AND MUSIC. IT WAS CHOREOGRAPHED BY BULAT AYUKHANOV.

ZHANIYA AUBAKIROVA, PIANIST LAUREATE AND DIRECTOR OF THE ALMATY CONSERVATORY,
CONDUCTS A MASTER PIANO CLASS WITH STUDENT ZHUMABEK BEKISHEV.

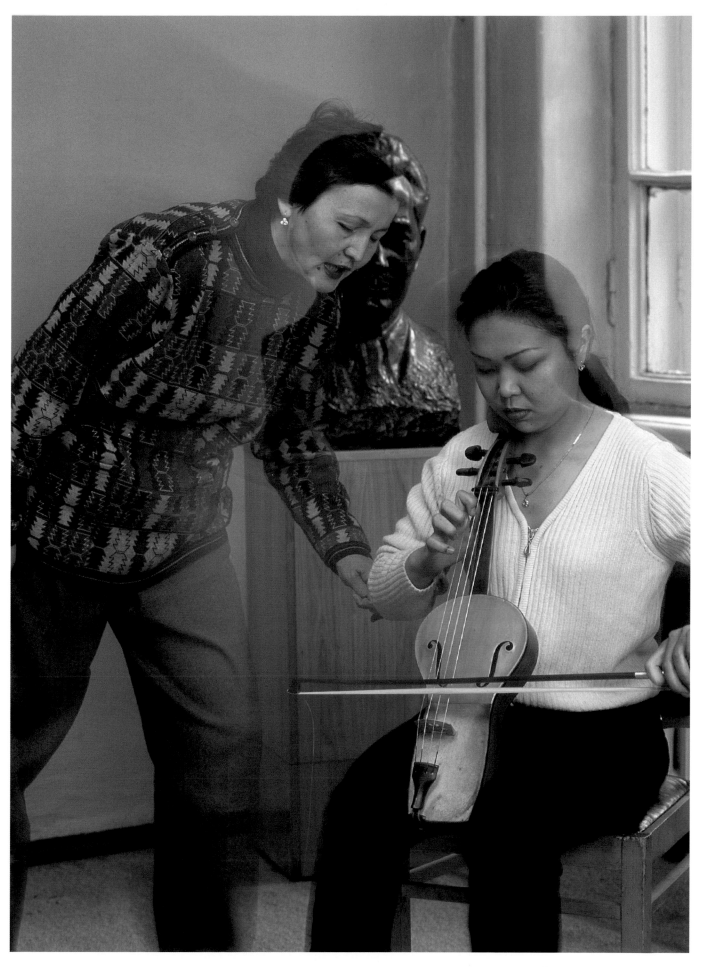

GALIA MOLDAKARIMOVA CONDUCTS A MASTER CLASS IN MODERN **QOBÏZ**, AN UPDATED VERSION OF THE
TRADITIONAL INSTRUMENT, AT THE ALMATY CONSERVATORY. HER STUDENTS ARE AINAGUL ISKAKOVA,
DINA MIRBEKOVA, JAZIRA AOUEZOVA, KENJEGUL MOUSAEVA AND BIBIGUL BATYRBEKOVA.

TUTOR NAZGUL ALIASKAROVA TEACHES YOUNG ENTHUSIASTS THE GUITAR AT THE ARKHIMED SCHOOL IN ALMATY.

COMPOSER EDWARD BOGUSHEVSKY PROVIDES TRADITIONAL KAZAKH HOSPITALITY AS WELL AS FOOD FOR THOUGHT IN A DISCUSSION OF MUSICAL PHILOSOPHY AT HIS HOME IN ALMATY. HE IS A POPULAR COMPOSER OF SCORES FOR CINEMA AND THEATER, WITH CREDITS FOR MORE THAN 150 FILMS AND 60 PLAYS. HE HAS ALSO DONE WHAT HE CALLS "ECOLOGICAL COMPOSITIONS" FOR NATURE AND ANIMAL FILMS.

A SERIES OF CONCERTS WAS HELD TO CELEBRATE THE 75TH BIRTHDAY OF RENOWNED CONDUCTOR FUAT MANSUROV. THESE
INCLUDED TRADITIONAL KAZAKH MUSIC AND INSTRUMENTS, SEEN HERE, AS WELL AS WESTERN ORCHESTRAL MUSIC, OPERA ARIAS,
INSTRUMENTAL SOLOISTS AND CHORAL WORKS AT CENTRAL CONCERT HALL, WHICH WAS FILLED TO OVERFLOWING.

"GULZIYA STAMBEKOVA, A STUDENT AT THE ALMATY CONSERVATORY, BRILLIANTLY PERFORMED "FLIGHT OF THE BUMBLE BEE" ON THE MODERN QOBÏZ, WITH FUAT MANSUROV CONDUCTING THE QURMANGHAZÏ ORCHESTRA. IN THE LAST FEW MEASURES ONE OF HER STRINGS BROKE. THE ORCHESTRA FINISHED THE LAST BARS, AND THE AUDIENCE BROKE INTO THUNDEROUS APPLAUSE AS MR. MANSUROV SWEPT HER UP AFTER HER BOWS AND CARRIED HER OFF THE STAGE OF THE CENTRAL CONCERT HALL." – W.E.

YOUNG ERBOLAT KURGANBEKOV IS A PRODIGY ON THE **QOBÏZ**, THE INSTRUMENT CREATED IN THE 8TH CENTURY BY QURQÏT-ATA. IT IS USED TO IMPROVISE MEDITATIVE AND SPIRITUAL MUSIC.

TALGAT MUKUSHEV, A MUSICIAN WITH THE QURMANGHAZÏ ORCHESTRA, PLAYS A TRADITIONAL **SÏBÏZGHÏ** (REED FLUTE) IN A SOLO PASSAGE. THE NATIONAL MUSICAL INSTRUMENTS ORCHESTRA WAS FOUNDED IN 1934 AS A **DOMBRA** ENSEMBLE AND NAMED FOR THE GREAT FOLK MUSICIAN. TODAY SOME OF THE INSTRUMENTS IN THE ORCHESTRA INCLUDE THE **QOBÏZ**, THE **SAZGEN**, THE **SYRNAI** AND THE **ZHETYGEN**. AN EXTENSIVE REPERTOIRE EMBRACES BOTH KAZAKH AND CLASSICAL MUSIC.

CENTURIES-OLD POEMS, ORAL LEGENDS AND MUSICAL FOLKLORE WERE THE SOURCE FOR MANY 20TH CENTURY PLAYS, OPERAS, BALLETS, SYMPHONIES AND LITERATURE. ÄUEZOV'S PLAY **ENLIK AND KEBEK**, BASED ON THE FOLK LEGENDS OF THE TRAGIC AND FAITHFUL YOUNG LOVERS, IS A PRIME EXAMPLE. IT IS PERFORMED HERE AT THE KAZAKH DRAMA THEATER, BIRTHPLACE OF KAZAKH PROFESSIONAL THEATER.

SELECTIONS FROM MUKHTAR ÄUEZOV'S PLAYS **SHOOT ON THE MOUNTAIN PASS**, **ENLIK AND KEBEK** AND **AYMAN-SHOLPAN**, A FOLKLORE-BASED MUSICAL, WERE PERFORMED AS PART OF THE ÄUEZOV JUBILEE FESTIVAL AT THE DOSTOYEVSKY THEATER IN SEMEY IN EASTERN KAZAKHSTAN.

AN ACTOR PORTRAYED MUKHTAR ÄUEZOV AT THE CELEBRATIONS COMMEMORATING HIS JUBILEE. THE RENOWNED WRITER, SCHOLAR AND TEACHER AUTHORED PLAYS, NOVELS, SHORT STORIES AND OPERA LIBRETTOS. HE WAS BORN IN THE SHYNGYSTAU HILLS SOUTH OF SEMEY, TERRITORY OF THE MIDDLE HORDE, WHOSE PEOPLE WERE KNOWN FOR THEIR ELOQUENCE. THIS WAS ALSO THE BIRTHPLACE OF NATIONAL POET ABAY QUNANBAY AND BARD SHAKARIM QUDAYBERDIEV.

COMPOSER ALMAS SERKEBAYEV FOOTNOTES HIS STIRRING AND MOVING COMPOSITION "THIS IS MY HOME," WHICH HE HAS JUST FINISHED PLAYING ON THE PIANO. HE COMPOSED THE SCORE FOR THE POPULAR **ASÀK-KULÀN**, WHICH WAS PERFORMED FOR NEARLY 10 YEARS BY THE KAZAKH STATE OPERA AND BALLET COMPANY, AS WELL AS SYMPHONIES, CONCERTOS AND A ROCK-OPERA-BALLET.

THIS UIGHUR FOLK DANCE AND MUSIC PERFORMANCE TOOK PLACE AT THE KAZAKH DRAMA THEATER IN ALMATY. THE UIGHURS, A TURKIC TRIBE WITH ITS OWN WRITTEN LANGUAGE, RULED IN TURKESTAN AND MONGOLIA IN THE 8TH TO 12TH CENTURIES. THE UIGHURS COOPERATED WITH CHINGIS KHAN'S TROOPS AND TAUGHT THEM TO WRITE USING UIGHUR SCRIPT. THEY BECAME SKILLED MERCHANTS, CRAFTSMEN AND TRADERS ALONG THE SILK ROAD INTO WESTERN CHINA.

POP SINGER ROZA RYMBAYEVA PERFORMS AT THE ÄUEZOV JUBILEE FESTIVAL IN SEMEY.

A MUSICAL PERFORMANCE WITH TRADITIONAL FOLK INSTRUMENTS AND COSTUMES TAKES PLACE IN A YURT IN THE VILLAGE OF SHIELI IN THE QÏZÏLORDA REGION.

THE KAZAKH STATE CIRCUS PERFORMANCES DRAW ON NATIONAL GAMES LIKE WRESTLING, ROPE CLIMBING AND HORSEMANSHIP. THE MAIN EVENT IS USUALLY A THRILLING SHOW OF HORSE-RIDING FEATS AND ACROBATICS. THIS SHOW WAS IN ALMATY.

KAZAKH FOLK DANCERS AND MUSICIANS PERFORM AT ZHIDEBAI IN NORTHEASTERN KAZAKHSTAN.

GULZHAN TUTKIBAEVA SEEMS TO DEFY GRAVITY IN HER STAGE ENTRANCE. SHE IS A PEOPLE'S
ARTIST OF THE REPUBLIC OF KAZAKHSTAN AND A PRIMA BALLERINA OF THE KAZAKH STATE
THEATER OF OPERA AND BALLET, ALSO KNOWN AS THE ABAY THEATER OF OPERA AND BALLET.

## RITES AND PASSAGES: THE CIRCLE OF LIFE

The life of a human from birth to death is, in essence, a chain of transitions from one state to another, from one age and social group to another. Kazakhs measure the human life through the *müshel*, a 12-year animal cycle.

The first of these cycles begins the day the child reaches the age of one – the end of the first year of life. The first year is considered to mark the child's transition from nonexistence to existence. All the significant transitions over the course of a person's life are marked by special rites and holidays, and they are especially rich in number and meaning during the first year of a child's life.

In the past if a child was born prematurely, he or she would be placed in the fur cap of the grandfather. The parents would then hang the cap on the uppermost fork of the lattice framework of the yurt. Over the course of 40 days the baby was cared for and moved one fork each day around the interior of the yurt until the infant's health was assured.

Parents would seek the birth of a healthy baby by untying all knots, opening the lids of all trunks and undoing the braids of the birthing mother, magical actions traditionally believed to benefit her. A young, happily married woman would then cut the newborn's umbilical cord, or *kindik*, and serve as the child's second mother or godmother – the baby's *kindik sheshe* or, literally, umbilical-cord mother. On the third or seventh day – auspicious days based on "magical" numbers – the child was placed in a *besik*, or cradle, which had been cleansed earlier with the fire and smoke of burning juniper, sage or wild rue. The baby's first garment and utensils evoke an allegory. The newly sewn garment, called an *it köylek*, or dog shirt, was first placed symbolically on a puppy. Later the child's dish was referred to as an *it ayaq*, or dog bowl. Behind all of this was an allegorical appeal to the wolf, the totem of the Kazakhs, to protect the child, and an effort to confuse evil spirits who might threaten the baby's life.

The child's first independent steps indicate that he or she is ready to enter the world of adults and the occasion is marked with the rite of *tusau kesu*, or cutting the cord. The feet of the child were tied with an *ala zhip*, or motley string, woven of black and white woolen threads. Then a woman known for her swiftness and success cuts the strings, "freeing" the child and symbolically sending him or her on the path of life with wishes for great success. Later, one end of that string is attached to a kerchief filled with sweets, and the other end to the neck of a puppy. The child runs after the puppy with noisy laughter and collects the sweets that spill out, while the mother gathers the hobbles of the *tusau* and keeps them her whole life as a memento together with the child's first outfit, much as a Western mother will keep or "bronze" a baby's first shoes.

From the ages of two to seven a male child undergoes two additional important rites of passage. One is the *sündet-toy*, or circumcision, which marks his acceptance into the Islamic community. The other is *atqa minggizu*, or mounting the horse, which welcomes the boy into the nomadic world. In the latter rite, a special child's saddle called an *ashatay*, which is heavily ornamented and has high pommels, is prepared for the initiate and the steed is outfitted with a beautiful horse-

20TH-CENTURY SADDLE POMMEL

cloth. The boy, dressed in new clothes, leads the horse by the bridle to visit relatives and close friends and invites everyone to a celebration. They congratulate the youngster, give him gifts, and on the next day they all gather for a feast. The *naghashï* – literally mother's brother, or maternal uncle – who has a special status among the Kazakhs, presents the boy with his first horse, just as he earlier presented the child's crib.

In the relationship with his *naghashï*, the *zhiyen*, or nephew, had higher claim to the uncle's attention than did his own children. Uncles always try to fulfill their nephews' requests and support them as much as possible. This formed a traditional, multilayered social protection for the child from the lines of both the mother and the father, like the two wings of a bird.

The Kazakhs' love of children is expressed in many different ways. The nomad expresses his affection for children by diminutive endearments such as *qozïm* (my lamb), *qulïnïm* (my little camel) or *zharïghïm* (my light). It was not considered acceptable to kiss children since kissing was reserved for marriage. Instead adults nuzzle the child's forehead while whispering *aynalayïn*. This word, which literally means "let me go around you," is one of the most poignant, affectionate and tender expressions a Kazakh can use. It goes back to the shamans' practice of circling the person who is ill to draw the illness to himself and in an effort to protect the patient from evil spirits. In an affectionate manner *aynalayïn* is heard as a request to the Almighty: "May all difficulties fall upon my head. I am ready to sacrifice myself for the sake of your well-being." In addition to protection, children are given respect. Even young children are accepted as rational and autonomous beings whose rights are to be considered. The boy is seen as a future leader, and the girl as a guest at home and a future mother. Kazakhs believe in bringing up individuals to be proud and independent, and this requires respect from early childhood.

Towards the end of the first

ALTÏBAQAN, NOMADIC-STYLE SWING

*müshel*, or 12-year cycle – in other words, by age 13 – the children are expected to have mastered all of the basic skills of tending to livestock and keeping a household, and they have gradually learned what their individual talents and inclinations are. Participating in mounted sports competitions known as *bäyge* and horse races over long distances (from 3 to 5 kilometers to as far as 50 kilometers) were the dreams of every young boy. Such skills required a trained body and knowledge of the peculiarities of horses, as well

ARGUVAN, GRANDSON OF ABSENT, AN OLYMPIC CHAMPION AKHAL-TEKE HORSE

as a complete "oneness" with them.

The period of the second *müshel* is the time of blossoming youth and freedom, a time filled with games and competitions.

Especially noteworthy are the youth gatherings known as *bastanghï*, or beginnings, in which unmarried adolescents whose parents have gone to visit a neighboring settlement, "play" at being adults. Chaperoned by all the daughters-in-law of the village, they invite each other over for company, prepare food and in general imitate the behavior and even the intonations of adult conversation. By filling the vacuum left by the absent adults and replicating the structure of traditional society, these gatherings allowed the individual talents of the youth to bloom and be seen in all their beauty. It often revealed future leaders, and in its own way prepared participants for the adult lives they would soon lead.

The zenith of this period of life was the wedding – that most serious and joyous of social transitions – and every step was carefully regulated and deeply symbolic. Kazakhs pay particular attention to the origins of the *qalïngdïq*, or bride – the future mistress of the hearth – because they believe that only individuals who have grown up in good families can establish good families. Thus, the responsibility for the right choice belongs to the elders. Kazakhs have a saying – "Bridegrooms are for a hundred years, but in-laws are for a thousand years" – which expresses the idea that a marriage unites not just two individuals, but two clans or tribes. It is only with the establishment of a family that the system of kinship is fully realized. It's no wonder there is the saying: "Each person has three sets of relatives: his father's relatives, his mother's relatives, and his in-laws."

It is interesting to note here that a central point in the campaign of the Soviets to "liberate the women of the East" was to abolish the *qalïng mal*, or bride price. This misguided effort completely ignored the economic and social point of the bride price. According to tradition, the size of the bride price paid by the groom's family was to be equal to the dowry of the bride, which included her own fully furnished yurt together with all of the necessary accessories, clothing and decorations. This dowry guaranteed the new bride social independence in the new world of her husband's family, and also recognized her rights in that the dowry remained her personal property and would be inherited by her children.

The procession of the bride to her new home accompanied by her relatives and girlfriends is still an unforgettable sight that symbolizes the most important transitional rite – the bride's "death" as a girl and her "rebirth" as a woman in a new place and role. While abandoning the home of her birth and childhood, the girl cries and sings the song of farewell known as the *sïngsu*. At the home of her new husband she is welcomed by what is even today the most popular wedding song, known as the *zhar-zhar*, which is performed as an upbeat dialogue between separate groups of male and female singers.

This long chain of rituals helps the bride to cross the threshold of her new world. The bride is met by her *ene*, or mother-in-law, who

– just as in the rituals surrounding adoption – holds a loaf of warm bread to her bosom to show that her heart is ready to love her new daughter. The bride bows in reverence to the fire of the new hearth (and thus worships it) and kindles the flame by pouring fat on it as an offering to the spirits of the ancestors. The smoke cleanses the bride and joins her to the new family. After the presentation of the bride to the Upper World – the world of the ancestors – she is introduced to the world of her new relatives through the ceremony known as *betashar*, or the unveiling of the bride. In his wedding song, the bard-improviser sings an admonition to the young bride, instructing her about the rules of family life and describing all the members of the new family. Then two women lift the veil covering the bride, and she bows to each new relative, who offer her a *körimdik*, a gift for having seen and met her. Later the bride confers upon each one of them her own affectionate nicknames, avoiding words that are similar to or sound like the given names of her in-laws. This demonstrates the depth and power of these "Words and Good Wishes."

For the young, weddings are a time for games and competitions; and among Kazakhs the most beloved game is *qïz quu*, or chasing the girl. Smartly dressed girls of marriageable age arrive on prancing horses before a group of single young men on horseback. They joke and exchange witticisms until, with gentle lashes of a whip, each girl indicates which

boy she has chosen to challenge to a competition. The young male rider then chases the girl on horseback and tries to kiss her. If he is not able to do so (or if she does not permit him to!), the girl then chases the young man back and lashes him with a *qamshï*,

COMPETITOR IN THE GAME OF QÏZ QUU

or whip, to embarrass him.

During weddings, a number of games on horseback are played. There are horse races known as *bäyge*, competitions on pacers called *zhorgha zharïs*, jousting, and shooting at a target with a bow or firearm at full gallop. Often there is also wrestling. The competition known as *kümis alu* or *tenge alu* (grabbing a coin) demands the dexterity of a circus equestrian as young men try to grab coins fastened to a kerchief or even scattered on the ground. A game of dethronement, called *audarïspaq*, is a worthy spectacle as two riders on horseback attempt to topple one another from the saddle.

The most dynamic form of horseback competition is *kökpar*, also known as *buzkashi*. It literally means "goat grab," and in it, up to 30 riders – usually mature men – participate. The contest centers around the headless carcass of a two-year-old goat, and the aim is to use riding skills and aggressive strength to transport it from the place of the competition to one's own home. Excited screams and dust rise up to the sky, and spectators are treated to unbridled passion, clear horrors, the neighing and rearing of charging horses and the awesome strength and agility of the riders. In this striking game, more than a goat is at stake since winning is a potent symbol of sexual prowess and leadership as well. This game also takes place during the *as*, or annual feast, and not by coincidence. Competitive ritual games like this one have always taken place when large numbers of participants gather for inter-tribal events – usually weddings and feasts – intensifying the test and making victory all the sweeter.

Competitiveness became literally the soul and flesh of the culture, permeating it through and through, much as it did for the ancient Greeks. This is seen in the many types of dueling competitions, sports on horseback, and the competitive games played by adults, youths of both genders and children. It is even reflected in the remarkable range of traditional Kazakh songs, rites, rituals and customs, especially songs performed as a dialogue or in a question-and-answer form. To a certain degree, these competitions equalized all social, gender and age groups of society. Even such an inviolable member of the family and the social group as the head of household could be drawn into a game with a child through witty provocation. A unique Kazakh aphorism says, "If you find the right words, you can even get your father to play."

These Kazakh holidays and games help to define one more significant lesson from the nomadic tradition: Competitions not only teach a youth that victory is to win fairly at any cost, but also the importance of being worthy in defeat – to know how to control oneself, to regulate emotions and rein in aggression, to observe the rules of a game, and to learn the art of leaving a complicated and unfavorable situation with a disarmingly humorous phrase that preserves one's dignity. These social skills formed indispensable tools for coexisting harmoniously within a traditional society. The rules of the *aytïs*, or word duels between bards, address this delicate balance as well: The losing poet is given the opportunity to retain his dignity and show his mastery by reciting from memory the entire *aytïs*, including all of its dialogues – a challenging feat worthy of a victor.

The end of the second *müshel* – at the age of 25 – is considered to be a defining boundary line in a person's life. This marks the culmination of freedom and at the same time the loss of youth. There is not a poet or singer in Kazakhstan who has not composed a wistful song in the special genre known as *qoshtasu*, or song of farewell. The poetry of the *qoshtasu* is filled with a keen sense of the swift passage of time and the fleeting nature of existence. However bidding farewell to youth also means welcoming the ripening and fullness of maturity when, over the course of the next 24 years (two 12-year *müshel* cycles), carefree young people become parents, teach their children to walk, ride and work, and help them to build their own families. This is a period of productivity, achievement and fruitfulness when knowledge combined with strength "brings forth the catch," as hunters say. And one of the clearest and strongest symbols of this period in life *is* the art of hunting.

Hunting is both sport and food-gathering. Often, mature men will take part in collective hunts known as *salburïn*, especially using hunting birds. The basic hunting bird is not so much the falcon as in Europe and the Middle East, but rather the eagle, or *bürkit*. About 10 different kinds of hawks are also trained. The complicated art of taming a bird of prey to hunt was hardly possible for everyone to master; thus Kazakhs call a hunter with eagles a *qusbegi*, or Lord of the Birds. His relationship to his bird of prey – especially to the eagle – is almost mystical. Ancient nomads could not help but be amazed by the intelligence, the fierce courage, and the physical strength of the eagle – its command of its realm and its proximity to the sky and the sun. Even the eagles' nests situated high in the mountains confirm their natural, lofty status. Many features distinguish the eagle from the fauna surrounding it, especially the fact that the eagle would easily take on a fox, wolf, deer or ram, but would never attack a human being. People were struck even more by the frightening appearance of the eagle – eyes blazing with fire and, as the early Kazakhs believed, able to command thunderbolts. All these qualities meant the eagle was close to being a divinity – or more specifically, a goddess. The female eagle is stronger and more fearless, and thus is preferred for hunting.

Everything connected with the eagle was magical: its feathers; its talons, which were used as an amulet; the leather hood; the roost upon which it sat inside the yurt (often a tree trunk dug into the ground); and the forked wooden perch, known as a *baldaq,* upon which the bird sat upon the hand of the hunter riding to the hunt. Birthing mothers would bring into the yurt either an eagle or objects related to it in order to scare away the mythical Qaraqus or "Black Bird," which might steal the spirit of the newborn child. An eagle or other bird of prey was often kept in the yurt by a childless couple in the belief that the mere presence of such a bird increased fertility.

A trained eagle and its owner form an indivisible pair. A Kazakh's relationship with his eagle can only be compared with the relationship with his horse – caring, affectionate, anxious and loving. After 10 or 12 years of faithful service the owner frees the eagle to allow it to have its own family so that it can bring new birds of prey into the world and start a new cycle in its own, now airborne, life.

Thus it is through eternal circles – the circle of the sun, of the open steppe, of the yurt's design, of the ornamental horned scroll and of the cycle of the *müshels* – that the life of a Kazakh also passes. The completion of one circle means the beginning of the next. And each moment of transition is consciously and carefully marked by the appropriate customs, rituals and holidays.

One of these principle annual cycles is marked by the beginning of the traditional new year, which occurs on the day of the vernal equinox, March 21 or 22. Naurïz, which means "New Day" in Persian, is a national holiday, and variations of the traditional activities described here are still celebrated in some form even in urban settings today.

Holiday preparations fill days leading up to Naurïz: Homes are cleaned, new clothes are sewn, and the ingredients of special dishes are gathered. On the eve of Naurïz, a bonfire is lit and young people jump over it and people wander about with torches. Women gather to cook *naurïz közhe,* a soup made of seven ingredients: water, salt, meat, wheat, millet, rice and milk. While stirring the soup in a large pot, the women sing songs and pronounce blessings. At sunrise, the community sits down to its first meal of the new year eating *naurïz közhe* and wishing each other a long life. Then they call upon relatives, who await them with spreads of delicious food.

Elders, first, are offered the delicacy of boiled sheep's head, songs are sung, *küy* songs are played and bards engage in verbal dueling competitions. Horse competitions follow – usually *bäyge* and *kökpar.* Young people erect festive swings called *altïbaqan* and play games late into the night, especially the popular Aqsüyek, or White Bone. This game involves couples looking for a sheep's tibia bone that has been thrown out into the open steppe, into a magical night full of laughter and freedom and touching under a spring sky filled with stars.

The holiday, which is a short but joyous respite on the path of life, quiets down and a new morning arises in the endless steppe, signifying yet another beginning, yet another rebirth.

A HELIANTHUS BLOSSOM

It is a rebirth in which Kazakhs believe wholeheartedly, a belief that carries us through snowstorms and intense heat, through losses and disappointments, through betrayals and challenges and all the tests of fate that lead into the future.

Now, just inside the door of a new millennium, mindful of all the trials and tribulations we have overcome, all the tears and joys of living, all the successes and victories, and all the promise of the future, the greatest weight we Kazakhs carry with us on our path forward are the three great pillars of truth given to us by a shared history: First is *Experience* – the lessons of the past; then *Memory* – the thread that guides us on our path; and finally *Hope* – our inexhaustible source of strength.

I believe in the immortality of the Soul of Kazakhstan.

*– Alma Kunanbay*

ETERNAL FLAME, PANFILOV PARK, ALMATY

A YOUNG COUPLE IN MODERN VERSIONS OF TRADITIONAL WEDDING ATTIRE PREPARE FOR THEIR MARRIAGE CEREMONY. A BRIDE'S DRESS IS OFTEN CONSIDERED THE ZENITH OF THE DRESSMAKER'S ART. HER HEADDRESS IS CALLED A SÄUKELE, AND ITS DESIGN AND ORNA- MENTATION ARE LADEN WITH MANY LEVELS OF MEANING AND SYMBOLISM.

DURING THE CEREMONY, MUSICIANS BEGIN TO PLAY TRADITIONAL INSTRUMENTS WHILE THEY RECITE THE BRIDE'S LINEAGE. SHE BOWS EACH TIME THE SINGER CALLS OUT THE NAME OF AN ANCESTOR.

NURSULU AYTANOVA WITH YOUNG BEKNUR AND AMANGELDY WHO ARE GUESTS AT THE WEDDING IN SHIELI.

THE BRIDE, RAUSHAN AUEZOVA, POURS FAT ONTO THE FIRE IN THE VILLAGE OF SHIELI IN THE QÏZÏLORDA REGION. IT IS CONSIDERED AN ACT OF CLEANSING AS WELL AS AN OFFERING TO ANCESTORS, AND IT MARKS THE BEGINNING OF THE CEREMONY.

RAUSHAN AUEZOVA, THE BRIDE, AND HER ATTENDANTS MADINA AND SHYNAR BEGIN THE "UNVEILING OF THE BRIDE," THE PART OF THE WEDDING CALLED THE **BETASHAR**, AT A TRADITIONAL CEREMONY.

CLAN MATRIARCHS IN SHIELI (LEFT TO RIGHT) DARKHAN SADENOVA, SHADAN TONBETOVA, MANAP MYKHANOVA AND ULJAN SAMETOVA GATHER TO JOIN IN THE JOYOUS RITUALS OF PRESENTING THE BABY IN THE CRADLE AND CUTTING THE CORD.

BESIKKE SALU, OR "PUTTING IN THE CRADLE," IS A CEREMONY FOR BLESSING A NEW BABY. THIS ENTAILS PLACING THE INFANT IN ITS CRADLE AND, TO ENSURE BLESSINGS, PUTTING A SMALL MIRROR OR BRUSH UNDER THE PILLOW FOR A BABY GIRL OR A WHIP AND KNIFE FOR A BOY. A BURNING SPRIG OF SAGE OR A FLAME, AS PICTURED HERE, IS PASSED OVER THE CRADLE AS A SYMBOL OF CLEANSING, LIFE AND PROTECTION. A GRANDMOTHER THEN PINCHES THE BABY'S NOSE TO MAKE IT CRY, WHICH ASSURES A CALM, DEEP SLEEP AFTERWARDS. ARAILYM SAMETOVA IS THE BABY BEING BLESSED HERE. HER MOTHER, GULMARZHAN IKHANOVA, IS AT LEFT, AND THE GODMOTHER, GALIYA USENBAEVA, IS THE YOUNG WOMAN BEHIND THE CRADLE.

TUSAU KESU, OR "CUTTING THE CORD," IS A RITE THAT MARKS THE PASSAGE OF A CHILD FROM INFANT TO TODDLER STAGE. IN THE CEREMONY, A BRAIDED BLACK AND WHITE WOOL STRING IS TIED TO THE CHILD'S ANKLES, AND THE MOTHER CHOOSES A WOMAN RESPECTED FOR HER GOOD QUALITIES AND SUCCESS TO CUT THE CORD. THIS SYMBOLICALLY FREES THE CHILD AND SENDS HIM OR HER ON THE PATH OF LIFE WITH BLESSINGS AND GOOD WISHES. THE CEREMONY PICTURED ABOVE, IN SHIELI, IS FOR YOUNG SALTANAT AMANGELDIEVA.

THESE YOUNG BOYS ENTERTAIN THEMSELVES AT A WEDDING WITH A GAME CALLED **ASYKS**, IN WHICH AN ODD NUMBER OF SHEEP BONES, OR **ASYKS**, ARE PLACED IN A ROW. THE OBJECT IS TO DEMONSTRATE A FAST HAND AND A SHARP EYE BY KNOCKING OFF AS MANY BONES AS POSSIBLE. SYMBOLICALLY, THE MORE BONES YOU COLLECT THE MORE SHEEP YOU WILL HAVE.

A YOUNG DANCER TAKES A BREAK AT A TRADITIONAL PERFORMANCE IN PANFILOV PARK NEAR DOWNTOWN ALMATY.

TENGE-ALU, OR "PICKING UP COINS," IS A GAME IN WHICH A HANDKERCHIEF IS FILLED WITH MONEY AND PLACED ON THE GROUND.
A SKILLED RIDER GALLOPS AT BREAKNECK SPEED, LEANS DOWN AND TRIES TO SNATCH UP THE PRIZE.

KAZAKH HORSEMEN HAVE
EARNED A REPUTATION
AS SKILLED AND POWERFUL
RIDERS THAT STRETCHES
BACK GENERATIONS AND
MILLENNIA. CHILDREN
START RIDING WHEN THEY
ARE AROUND THREE YEARS
OLD. IN THIS **BÄYGE**
CONTEST, YOUNG MEN RACE
EACH OTHER OVER RUGGED
TERRAIN FOR A PRESET
DISTANCE. FURIOUS, WILD,
EXUBERANT AND
FEARLESS – THESE ARE THE
CHARACTERISTICS OF
KAZAKH HORSEMANSHIP.

QÏZ QUU, OR "CHASING THE GIRL," IS ANOTHER WELL-LOVED HORSEBACK GAME. IF THE BOY WINS THE RACE, HE GETS TO KISS THE GIRL ON THE RIDE BACK TO THE STARTING LINE. IF THE GIRL WINS, SHE GETS TO "WHIP" THE BOY ON THE RIDE BACK. THIS GAME TOOK PLACE IN THE VILLAGE OF ZHIDEBAI.

KÖKPAR IS A DRAMATIC GAME IN WHICH TWO GROUPS OF 15-20 RIDERS EACH STRUGGLE TO KEEP POSSESSION OF A TWO-YEAR-OLD HEADLESS GOAT. THE WINNING TEAM IS AWARDED A FEAST OF THE GOAT. IT IS ALSO KNOWN AS BUZKASHI, AND A VARIATION IS TO TRY TO PROPEL THE GOAT CARCASS FROM THE PLACE OF COMPETITION TO ONE'S OWN HOME. THE GAME IS PLAYED ON SPECIAL OCCASIONS LIKE THIS FESTIVAL IN THE VILLAGE OF ZHIDEBAI, AND IS ANOTHER CONTEST THAT WAS TRADITIONALLY INTENDED TO STRENGTHEN A WARRIOR'S SKILLS.

IN **AUDARÏSPAQ**, THE GOAL IS TO PULL YOUR OPPONENT OUT OF HIS SADDLE. MANY OF THE GAMES, SUCH AS THIS WRESTLING MATCH ON HORSEBACK IN SHIELI, WERE ORIGINALLY INTENDED TO IMPROVE ONE'S STRENGTH AND ABILITY AS A WARRIOR.

GOLDEN EAGLES – CALLED **BÜRKIT** IN KAZAKH – ARE TRAINED BY THEIR OWNERS FROM THE TIME THEY ARE CHICKS
TO BE HUNTERS. THIS ONE MEASURES MORE THAN 104 CENTIMETERS (41 INCHES) FROM THE TIP OF ITS BILL TO THE END OF ITS TAIL.
ITS WING SPAN MEASURES TWO METERS, OR MORE THAN SIX FEET. THESE POWERFUL BIRDS CAN KILL DEER, FOX AND WOLVES.
ONCE PLENTIFUL IN CENTRAL ASIA, THEY ARE NOW BECOMING RARE.

"ABDULKHAK TURLYBAYEV IS
KNOWN AS 'THE EAGLE MAN'
BECAUSE OF HIS MASTERY
OF THESE MAGNIFICENT
CREATURES. KAZAKHS CALL
MEN LIKE MR. TURLYBAYEV
'QUSBEGI,' OR 'LORD OF THE
BIRDS.' WATCHING HIM WORK
WITH HIS EAGLE QUICKLY
MADE ME UNDERSTAND
THAT WHAT HE HAS AND
FEELS TRANSCENDS 'SKILL'
– IT RISES TO 'RELATIONSHIP.'
KAZAKHS REVERE THE
GOLDEN EAGLE IN PART
BECAUSE THEY FLY SO HIGH
AND CLOSE TO THE SUN.
PILOTS HAVE REPORTED
SEEING THEM AS HIGH AS
20,000 FEET." – W.E.

THESE SCENES IN ZENKOV CATHEDRAL REFLECT THE FACT THAT FAITHS OF ALL PEOPLES ARE ONCE AGAIN FREE TO BE PRACTICED AND ARE DRAWING PEOPLE BACK TO ISLAM, CHRISTIANITY, JUDAISM, SHAMANISM, SUFISM, TENGRISM AND ZOROASTRIANISM THROUGHOUT THE COUNTRY.

SVYATO-VOZNESENSKY
CATHEDRAL IS COMMONLY
CALLED ZENKOV CATHEDRAL
AFTER ITS BUILDER, ANDRE
ZENKOV. THIS RUSSIAN
ORTHODOX EDIFICE IS IN
ALMATY'S PANFILOV PARK.
ITS CONSTRUCTION, BEGUN
IN 1904, IS ENTIRELY OF
WOOD WITHOUT THE USE
OF NAILS. IT WAS USED AS A
NATURAL HISTORY MUSEUM
DURING THE SOVIET ERA.
AT 56 METERS (184 FEET),
IT IS ONE OF THE TALLEST
WOODEN BUILDINGS IN
THE WORLD. IT SURVIVED
THE EARTHQUAKE OF 1911
THAT DEVASTATED ALMATY.

A YOUNG GIRL WATCHES THE END OF A WEDDING CEREMONY WHILE WAITING FOR HER BAPTISM TO BEGIN IN ZENKOV CATHEDRAL.

A TABLE IS LADEN WITH BREAD AND EGGS AT THE CHRISTMAS CHURCH OF CHRIST THE SAVIOR, A PARISH CHURCH IN ALMATY, FOR A "GOOD NEWS" SERVICE BEFORE EASTER.

TODAY ONE CAN SEE STRIKING IMAGES OF CHURCH AND STATE IN TOLERANCE OF EACH OTHER. ONE EXAMPLE IS THE SHARING OF IMPORTANT EVENTS LIKE THIS COMMEMORATIVE CEREMONY FOR FALLEN WORLD WAR II WARRIORS AT THE GLORY MEMORIAL IN PANFILOV PARK.

PARISHIONERS BRING CAKES AND DECORATED EGGS TO BE BLESSED AT RUSSIAN ORTHODOX EASTER SERVICES.

THIS HANDSOME, MODERN MOSQUE IN ALMATY WAS GIVEN TO THE PEOPLE OF KAZAKHSTAN BY EGYPT AND ITS PRESIDENT, HOSNI MUBARAK. THE EGYPTIANS ALSO ARE HELPING PLAN AN ISLAMIC UNIVERSITY COMPLEX AROUND THIS MOSQUE.

MUSLIM WOMEN PRAY AT
THE ÄUEZOV JUBILEE
CELEBRATIONS AT BORLI-AUL
IN EASTERN KAZAKHSTAN.

"THIS SACRED SITE OVERLOOKS LAKE BURABAY IN NORTHERN KAZAKHSTAN. OQZHETPES, THE STARK ROCK FORMATION IN THE BACKGROUND, MEANS, 'THE ARROW CANNOT REACH THIS PLACE.' THE LEGEND AS TOLD TO US RELATES THAT WHEN ABÏLAY KHAN WAS FIGHTING THE OYRATS, HIS ARMY CAMPED BELOW THIS ROCKY HILL. THE TROOPS CAPTURED A BEAUTIFUL PRINCESS AND THE KHAN DECREED THAT SHE WOULD MARRY A KAZAKH. SHE AGREED TO ACCEPT THE MAN WHO COULD SHOOT AN ARROW TO THE TOP OF THE HILL. ALL FAILED ON THE FIRST ATTEMPT. ON THE SECOND TRY, HER TRUE LOVE'S ARROW REACHED THE TOP. THE OTHERS WERE SO ENRAGED THAT THEY KILLED HIM. THE ANGUISHED PRINCESS THREW HERSELF INTO LAKE BURABAY WHERE SHE TURNED INTO THE SPHINX-LIKE ROCK FORMATION THAT PROTRUDES FROM THE WATER TO THIS DAY." – W.E.

A TREE BY AN ISOLATED MOUNTAIN STREAM IS COVERED BY PRAYER CLOTHS. THEY REPRESENT THE KAZAKH BELIEF THAT THE TREE OF LIFE CONNECTS MOTHER EARTH AND THE GREAT SPIRIT. PEOPLE ALWAYS CHOOSE TREES NEAR WATER – ESPECIALLY MOVING WATER – AND OFTEN IN THE MOUNTAINS, FOR THIS RITUAL. BOTH FACTORS ARE BELIEVED TO BRING THE PRAYERS NEARER TO GOD.

"PRAYER CLOTHS ON THIS MEMORIAL IN NARYNKOL NEAR THE SACRED MOUNTAIN KHAN-TENGRI VENERATE RAIYMBEK, A KAZAKH WARRIOR WHO FOUGHT THE DZUNGARS (MONGOLS) IN THE 1700S. HIS NAME BECAME A BATTLE CRY FOR HIS TRIBE, THE ALBAN. WE CAME UPON THIS MEMORIAL ON THE DAY BEFORE WE WERE TO RETURN TO THE UNITED STATES AFTER FINISHING OUR LAST SHOOT, FITTINGLY, AT THE SUMMIT OF KHAN-TENGRI. I HAD CARRIED A PRAYER CLOTH WITH ME DURING THE YEAR WE PHOTOGRAPHED IN KAZAKHSTAN AND STILL HAD IT WITH ME. I TIED MY PRAYER CLOTH TO THE MEMORIAL; AND AS MY WIFE, PATTI, AND I DROVE AWAY, A DOUBLE-RAINBOW FORMED OVER THE STEPPES, A FITTING MARKER AFTER A REMARKABLE YEAR OF DISCOVERY." – W.E.

255

"THE AFTERNOON WE SPENT PHOTOGRAPHING THE TEMPLE AT SHAKBAK-ATA, WE WERE PRIVILEGED TO WATCH A WONDERFUL RITUAL UNFOLD. IN THE VALLEY JUST BELOW US, CRAFTSMEN WERE COMPLETING A LOVELY NEW MAUSOLEUM. AS THEY LAID THE FINAL PIECE OF GLEAMING WHITE MARBLE IN PLACE, A BUS PULLED UP. THIS IN ITSELF WAS A SURPRISE BECAUSE THE DRIVE TO THIS SITE WAS OVER AN EXTREMELY ROUGH AND ROCKY TRACK. OUT OF THE BUS POURED RELATIVES: MEN, WOMEN AND CHILDREN, HERE TO EXAMINE, APPROVE, ADMIRE AND VIDEOTAPE THE NEW MEMORIAL. AFTER THEY WERE SATISFIED WITH THEIR INSPECTION, THEY SET UP A SPOT TO COOK DINNER TO CELEBRATE THE COMPLETION OF THE MAUSOLEUM." – W.E.

THE RAM'S SKULL AND HORNS AT THE SULTAN AKE MOSQUE SIGNIFY A DESIRE FOR THE DECEASED TO BE AS CLOSE TO THE GREAT SPIRIT AS THE SHEEP AND GOATS THAT CLIMB HIGH IN THE MOUNTAINS.

MOUNTAIN SHEEP ARE REVERED BECAUSE THEY CAN CLIMB TO HEIGHTS WHERE THE AIR AND WATER ARE PURE AND THEY ARE CLOSE TO THE GREAT SPIRIT. STATUES OF THEM ARE USED ON TOMBS IN "CITIES OF ANCESTORS" LIKE THIS ONE IN KOSHKURT-ATA NEAR AKTAU AS SYMBOLS OF THIS RELATIONSHIP WITH GOD.

SPIRIT YURTS, LIKE THIS ONE AT KOSHKURT-ATA, TAKE ON A WIDE RANGE OF FORMS AND INCORPORATE POETRY, SCULPTURE AND PAINTING TO ILLUMINATE THE LIVES OF THOSE WHO HAVE PASSED ON. THESE "CITIES OF THE ANCESTORS" ARE IN LARGE MEASURE THE ARCHITECTURAL HERITAGE OF THE KAZAKH NOMADS. A STORY RECORDED BY THE HISTORIAN HERODOTUS PERHAPS BEST ILLUSTRATES THEIR POWER AND MEANING TO THE KAZAKHS. IN 513 B.C., DARIUS I, KING OF PERSIA, ATTACKED THE SCYTHIANS IN WHAT IS NOW KAZAKHSTAN. THEY CONTINUED TO PULL BACK, SETTING THE STEPPES AFIRE AS THEY WENT. FRUSTRATED, DARIUS SENT A MESSENGER TO THE SCYTHIANS TO ASK WHY THEY WOULD NOT STAND AND FIGHT. IDANTHYRSUS, THEIR RULER, RESPONDED WITH THIS THREAT: "I HAVE NEVER FLED FROM A MAN IN FEAR IN DAYS PAST OR NOW.... WE HAVE NEITHER CITIES NOR SOWN LAND FOR WHICH WE MIGHT FEAR.... BUT IF YOU NEEDS MUST COME TO A FIGHT WITH US QUICKLY, THERE ARE OUR FATHERS' GRAVES. FIND THEM AND TRY TO RUIN THEM, AND YOU WILL DISCOVER WHETHER WE WILL FIGHT YOU OR NOT."

ZAURE IMANKULOVA IS KNOWN AS "THE PEOPLE'S HEALER" IN THE VILLAGE OF POKROVKA. WHEN SHE WAS A YOUNG GIRL IN QÏZÏLORDA, RABBI LEVI SCHNEERSON TAUGHT HER. DURING HER UNIVERSITY STUDIES SHE BECAME A LEADER IN THE STUDENTS' COMMUNIST PARTY AND BEGAN TO ESPOUSE ATHEISM. YEARS LATER WHILE WORKING IN A CLINIC, SHE DISCOVERED SHE HAD HEALING POWERS BEYOND CONVENTIONAL MEDICAL PRACTICES AND WAS ABLE TO HEAL A NUMBER OF PATIENTS. A FEW MONTHS LATER IN A DREAM, A HOLY MAN FROM THE 17TH CENTURY TOLD HER THAT SHE MUST USE THIS SPECIAL GIFT TO HEAL PEOPLE. SHE MOVED TO POKROVKA AND FOLLOWED THAT ADMONITION.

RELATIVES RECITE MUSLIM PRAYERS DURING A RITUAL HONORING
THE 25TH ANNIVERSARY OF THE PASSING OF ZHANGIR
UMBETOV'S FATHER IN THE COUNTRYSIDE NEAR THE VILLAGE
OF POKROVKA IN SOUTHEASTERN KAZAKHSTAN.

KAZAKH TOMBS ARE OFTEN BUILT IN THE SHAPE OF A YURT IN
AN OPEN STYLE – ESSENTIALLY "SPIRIT YURTS." NEAR THIS ONE
IN KATON-KARAGAI, THERE WAS A POEM WRITTEN BY THE
CHILDREN OF KAKITAI KABDOL ULY, BORN OCTOBER 5, 1931,
PASSED ON, AUGUST 3, 1997:

DEAREST FATHER,
WITH YOUNG MIND AND BLOOMING SOUL
CRUEL LIFE IS SINGING ABOUT YOU ITS SAD SONG.
YOUR CHILDREN ARE FULL OF THOUGHTS ABOUT YOU,
AND MISS YOU.
AND THERE IS NO WAY THAT SMILES CAN BE RETURNED.
WHAT A PITY THAT DESTINY IS SHOWING ITS BLACK SIDE.
THERE IS NOBODY WHOM I CAN COMPLAIN TO ABOUT IT.
YOU, MY FATHER, ARE PROTECTING WITH YOUR SPIRIT
US, YOUR CHILDREN, THE CONTINUATION OF YOUR LIFE.

HONORING ANCESTORS IS AN IMPORTANT PRACTICE IN TRADITIONAL KAZAKH FAITHS. THE SACRIFICE OF A SHEEP AT
THE "TREE OF LIFE" WAS PART OF THE RITUAL TO MARK THE PASSING OF ZHANGIR UMBETOV'S FATHER. AFTERWARDS,
A PORTION OF THE MEAT OF THE SHEEP IS GIVEN TO EACH GUEST. THE RITUAL IS ABOUT THE AFFIRMATION OF LIFE
NOT LOSS, AND THE ACKNOWLEDGMENT THAT ONE'S SPIRIT LIVES ON.

# BIBLIOGRAPHY *

Aitmatov, Chingis. *The Day Lasts More than a Hundred Years.* Translated by John French. Bloomington and Indianapolis: Indiana University Press, 1988.

Akhinzhanov, Serzhan. *Kypchaki v istorii srednevekovogo Kazakhstana* [The Qypchaqs in the history of medieval Kazakhstan (in Russian, with English summary)]. Almaty: Ghylym, 1995.

Akiner, Shirin. *The Formation of Kazakh Identity: From Tribe to Nation-State.* London: Royal Institute of International Affairs, Russian and CIS Program, 1995.

Akishev, Alisher. *Iskusstvo i mifologiia Sakov* [The art and mythology of the Sakas (in Russian)]. Alma-Ata: Nauka, 1984.

Akishev, Kemal. *Kurgan Issyk: Iskusstvo Sakov Kazakhstana* [The Issyk Mound: The arts of the Sakas of Kazakhstan (in Russian, with English summary)]. Moscow: Iskusstvo, 1978.

Allworth, Edward A. "The Rediscovery of Central Asia: The Region Reflected in Two Collections of the New York Public Library." *Bulletin of the New York Public Library* 4, no. 2 (spring 1996): 95–124.

Amandyqov, Iakuda. *Zhambyl zhyrlaidy* [Zhambyl sings (in Kazakh)]. Almaty: Qazaqstan Kompozitorlar odaghy, 1996.

Aravin, P. *Dauletkerei i Kazakhskaia muzyka XIX veka* [Dauletkerei and Kazakh music of the 19th century (in Russian)]. Moscow: Sovetskii kompozitor, 1984.

———. *Stepnye sozvezdiia: Ocherki i etiudy o Kazakhskoi muzyke* [The constellation of the steppe: Essays and etudes on Kazakh music (in Russian)]. Alma-Ata: Zhalyn, 1978.

Argynbayev, Khalel. *Qazaq xalqynyng qoloneri* [Kazakh applied art (in Kazakh)]. Almaty:Öner, 1987.

Auezov, Mukhtar O. *Abai.* 2 vols. Translated into English by Lev Navrozov. Edited by H. Perham. Moscow: Foreign Language Publishing House, n.d.; published in an abridged English edition with no translator/editor (Moscow: Progress Publishers, 1975).

———. *Fierce Grey* (in Kazakh, Russian, and English). Compiled by D. D. Turkbenbayeva. Almaty: Zheti Zhargy, 1997.

Auezov, Murat, and Mirlan Karataev, eds. *Kochevniki: Estetika: Poznanie mira traditsionnym Kazakhskim iskusstvom* [Nomadic esthetics: Cognition of the world in traditional Kazakh art (in Russian)]. Alma-Ata: Ghylym, 1993.

Bacon, Elizabeth E. *Central Asians under Russian Rule: A Study in Culture Change.* Ithaca and London: Cornell University Press, 1966. (Fourth printing 1994.)

Baipakov, Karl, and Lev Erzakovich, comps. *Ceramics of Medieval Otrar* (in Kazakh, Russian, and English). Almaty:Öner, 1991.

———. *Drevnie goroda Kazakhstana* [The ancient cities of Kazakhstan (in Russian)]. Alma-Ata: Nauka, 1971.

Baipakov, Karl, and Rakip Nasyrov. *Along the Great Silk Road* (in Russian and English). Translated by Maria Velizhanina and Adel Tereschchenko. Edited by Olga Talanova. Compiled, with a preface, by Lubov Shabykina and Olga Talanova. Photography by Oleg Belyalov, Victor Likhanov, and Vladimir Morozov. Almaty: Kramds-reklama, 1991.

Basilov, Vladimir N., ed. *Nomads of Eurasia.* Translated by Mary Fleming Zirin. Los Angeles: Natural History Museum of Los Angeles County, 1989; distributed by University of Washington Press.

Bekkhozhina, Taliga, comp./ed. *Qazyna* [A treasure (in Kazakh)]. Almaty: Ghylym, 1972.

Benson, Linda, and Ingvar Svanberg. *China's Last Nomads: The History and Culture of China's Kazaks.* Armonk, N.Y.: M. E. Sharpe, 1998.

Berger, Patricia, Terese Tse Bartholomew, et al. *Mongolia: The Legacy of Chinggis Khan.* Photographs by Kazuhiro Tsuruta. London and New York: Thames and Hudson Inc. and Asian Art Museum of San Francisco, 1995.

Bisenova, Gafura. *Pesennoe tvorchetsvo Abaia* [The song legacy of Abai (in Russian)]. Almaty: Daik-Press, 1995.

Cagatay, Ergun. *Once upon a Time in Central Asia* (in Turkish, English, and Russian). Edited by Lale Öz. Istanbul: Tetragon Iletisim Hizmetleri A.S., 1996.

Chadwick, Nora Kershaw, and Victor M. Zhirmunsky. *Oral Epics of Central Asia.* London: Cambridge University Press, 1969.

Dernova, Varvara, comp./ed. *Narodnaia muzyka v Kazakhstane* [Folk music in Kazakhstan (in Russian)]. Alma-Ata: Kazakhstan, 1967.

Daurenbekov, Zhakau, and Edige Tursynov. *Qazaq baqsy-balgerleri* [Kazakh folk healers (in Kazakh)]. Almaty: Ana Tili, 1993.

Dzhanibekov, Uzbekali. *Ekho…Po sledam legendy o zolotoi dombre* [Echo…On the trail of the legendary golden dombra (in Russian)]. Alma-Ata:Öner, 1990.

———. *The Kazakh Costume* (in Kazakh, Russian, and English). Almaty: Öner, 1996.

———. *Kul'tura Kazakhskogo remesla* [The culture of Kazakh craft (in Russian)]. Alma-Ata: Qazaqstan, 1982.

Edwards, Elwyn Hartley. *The Encyclopedia of the Horse.* New York: Dorling Kindersley Limited, 1994.

Edwards, Mike. "A Broken Empire: Kazakhstan, Facing the Nightmare." *National Geographic* 183, no. 3 (March 1993): 2, 22–37.

———. "Searching for the Scythians." *National Geographic* 190, no. 3 (September 1996): 54–79.

Erzakovich, Boris. *Pesennaia kultura Kazakhskogo naroda: Muzykalno-istoricheskoe issledovanie* [Song culture of the Kazakhs: A musical-historical study (in Russian)]. Alma-Ata: Nauka, 1966.

———, ed. *Kazakhskii muzykalnyi folklor* [Kazakh musical folklore (in Kazakh and Russian)]. Alma-Ata: Ghylym/Nauka Kazakhskoi SSR, 1982.

———. *Qazaq khalqynyng ghashyqtyq anderi antologiiasy* [Anthology of Kazakh folk songs about love (in Kazakh and Russian)]. Almaty: Ghylym, 1994.

Esenuly, Aitzhan (Toqtaghanov). *Kyui: Tangirding Kubiri* [Kyui: Epistle of the Most High (in Kazakh)]. Almaty: TOO Daik-Press, 1996; published in Russian as *Kyui: Poslanie Vsevyshenego* (Almaty: Kokil, 1997).

Foltz, Richard C. *Religions of the Silk Road: Overland Trade and Cultural Exchange from Antiquity to the Fifteenth Century.* New York: St. Martin's Press, 1999.

Gabbeh. Directed and edited by Mohsen Makhmalbaf. Performances by Shaghayegh Djodat, Hossein Moharami. 35 mm, 76 min. MK2 Prods./Sanayeh Dasti, 1996.

Gerasimov, Georgii. *Pamiatniki arkhitektury doliny reki Kara-Kengir* [Architectural landmarks in the Kara-Kengir River Valley in Central Kazakhstan (in Russian)]. Alma-Ata: Kazakh SSR Academy of Sciences, 1957.

Hali, Awelkhan, Zengxiang Li, Karl W. Luckert. *Kazakh Traditions of China.* Lanham, Md.: University Press of America, 1998.

Harvey, Janet. *Traditional Textiles of Central Asia.* London: Thames and Hudson, 1996.

Herodotus. *The Histories.* Translated by David Grene. Chicago and London: University of Chicago Press, 1987.

Hopkirk, Kathleen. *Central Asia: A Traveller's Companion.* London: John Murray Ltd., 1993.

Hopkirk, Peter. *The Great Game: The Struggle for Empire in Central Asia.* New York: Kodansha America, Inc., 1994; originally published as *The Great Game: On Secret Service in High Asia* (London: John Murray Ltd., 1990).

Ibraeva, Karlygash. *Kazakhskii ornament* [Kazakh ornamental pattern (in Russian)]. Almaty:Öner, 1994.

Ismailov, Esmagambet. *Akyny: Monografiia o tvorchestve Zhambula i drugikh narodnykh akynov* [Aqyns: A study of the work of Dzhambul and other folk singers (in Russian)]. Alma-Ata: Nauka, 1957; published first in Kazakh as *Aqyndar* (Almaty, 1956).

Karakulov, Bulat. *Asyl mura: Nasledie. Muzykalno-etnografichicheskii sbornik* [The precious heritage: A musical-ethnographic collection (in Kazakh and Russian)]. Alma-Ata: Ghylym, 1981.

Kekilbaev, Abish. *Jambyl's Time: Life of a Century* (in Kazakh, Russian, and English). Compiled by Olga Talanova. Almaty:Öner, 1996.

Ketegenova, Altyn, ed. *Makpal: 100 songs* [Velvet: 100 songs (in Kazakh and Russian)]. Gathered, compiled, and transcribed by Mukan Tulebaev. Almaty: Zhalyn, 1979.

Khazanov, Anatoly M. *Nomads and the Outside World.* 2nd ed. Translated by Julia Crookenden. With a foreword by Ernest Gellner. Madison: University of Wisconsin Press, 1994.

Kidaish-Pokrovskaia, Nina, and Orazgul Nurmagambetova. *Qoblandy batyr: Kazakhskii geroicheskii epos* [Koblandy-batyr: A Kazakh heroic epic (in Russian and Kazakh)]. Moscow: Nauka, 1975.

King, John, John Noble, and Andrew Humphreys. *Central Asia.* Hawthorn, Australia: Lonely Planet, 1996.

*Kirghiz Komuz and Kazakh Dombra.* Recorded with commentary by Jean During, Paris, France. OCORA, 1997 (C 560121). Compact disc.

Kliashtornyi, Sergei, and Tursun Sultanov. *Letopis' trekh tysiacheletij* [Chronicles of the three millenniums (in Russian)]. Alma-Ata: Rauan, 1992.

Knystautas, Algirdas, and Vladimir Flint. *The Natural History of the USSR.* Translated by John S. Scott. New York: McGraw-Hill Book Company, 1987.

Kunanbaeva, Alma. "The Kazakh Zhyrau as the Singer of Tales." In *Ethnohistorische Wege und Lehrjahre eines Philosophen: Festschrift dedicated to Prof. Lawrence Krader,* edited by Dittmar Schorkowitz, 293–303. Frankfurt am Main: Peter Lang, 1995.

*Kurmangazy and the Music of the Great Steppe* (in Russian and Kazakh). Produced in Almaty by Saida Elemanova. Financed by Tulpar, the Public Fund for Traditional Music. 2 compact discs.

*Kurmangazy orkestri.* Performances by the Qurmanghazï Orchestra of Folk Instruments. Produced in Astana by S. Baiterekov and T. Alpiev. Compact disc.

Levin, Theodore. *The Hundred Thousand Fools of God: Musical Travels in Central Asia (and Queens, New York).* Bloomington: Indiana University Press, 1996.

Magauin, Mukhtar. *Kobyz i kop'e: Povestvovanie o Kazakhskikh akynakh i zhyrau XV–XVIII vekov* [Qobyz and the spear: On Kazakh aqyns and zhyraus of the 15th–17th centuries (in Russian)]. Translated from Kazakh by Pavel Kosenko. Alma-Ata: Zhazushy, 1970.

Maier, Frith. *Trekking in Russia and Central Asia: A Traveler's Guide.* Seattle, Washington: The Mountaineers, 1994.

Margulan, Alkei. *Kazakhskoc narodnoe prikladnoe iskusstvo* [Kazakh ornamental folk art (in Russian, with English summary)]. 3 vols. Almaty:Öner, 1986–94.

———, ed. *Drevniaia kul'tura tsentral'nogo Kazakhstana* [The ancient culture of central Kazakhstan (in Russian)]. Alma-Ata: Nauka, 1966.

Masanov, Nurbulat. *Kochevaia tsivilizatsiia Kazakhov* [The nomadic civilization of the Kazakhs (in Russian)]. Almaty: Sotsinvest; Moscow: Gorizont, 1995.

262

Masanov, Nurbulat, Marat Mukanov, et al. *Kazakhi: Istoriko-etnograficheskoe issledovanie* [The Kazakhs: An ethno-history (in Russian)]. Almaty: Kazakhstan, 1995.

Maslow, Jonathan. "Golden Horse of Turkmenistan." With contributions by Rosalind Mazzawi and Henri Moser. *Aramco World* (May/June 1997): 12–19.

Medoev, Alan. *Graviury na skalakh* [Rock engravings: Petroglyph drawings in Kazakhstan (in Russian, with English summary)]. Alma-Ata: Zhalyn, 1979.

*Melodies of Kazakhstan.* 16 mm, 20 min. Distributed by Educational & Television Films, London, 1972.

Mendikulova, Gulnara. *Istoricheskie sud'by Kazakhskoi diaspory* [The historical fortunes of the Kazakh diaspora (in Russian)]. Almaty: Ghylym, 1997.

*Molom.* Directed by Marie Jaoul de Poncheville. Performances by Tseded, Yondejunai. 35 mm, 93 min. France/Mongolia, 1995. Distributed by Norkat Company (1997).

*Mongolie: Chants Kazakh et tradition epique de l'Ouest* [Mongolia: Kazakh songs and the epic tradition of the West]. Produced by A. Desjacques. OCORA/Harmonia Mundi C 558 660. Compact disc.

Mukanov, Marat. *Kazakhskaia yurta* [The Kazakh yurt (in Russian)]. Alma-Ata: Kainar, 1981.

Mukhambetova, Asiya. "The Traditional Musical Culture of Kazakhs in the Social Context of the 20th Century." *World of Music* 37, no. 3 (1995): 66–83.

*Music of Kazakhstan I: Songs Accompanied on Dombra and Solo Kobyz.* Produced by M. Morita, Tokyo, Japan. King Records KICC 5166. Compact disc.

*Music of Kazakhstan II: Dombra Music of Kazakhstan and Songs Accompanied on Dombra.* Produced by M. Morita, Tokyo, Japan. King Records KICC 5199. Compact disc.

Mustafina, Raushan. *Predstavleniia, kul'ty, obriady u Kazakhov* [The worldview, customs and rituals of the Kazakhs (in Russian)]. Alma-Ata: Qazaq universiteti, 1992.

Nasyrov, Rakip, comp. *Turkestan: A Photo Album.* Kazakh text by S. Bakbergenov; Russian text by R. Nasyrov; English translation by N. Golikov. Photographs by K. Mustafin. Almaty:Ōner, 1993.

Nurgaliev, Rymgali, et al. *Abai: Entsiklopediia* [Abai: An encyclopedia (in Kazakh)]. Almaty: Qazaq entsiklopediiasy, Atamyra, 1995.

Nurmukhammedov, Nagim-Bek. *Ahmed Yasawi Architectural Complex* (in Kazakh, Russian, and English). Almaty:Ōner, 1988.

Nuskabaiuly, Zharylkasyn, and Uzbekali Zhanibek, comps. *Ancient Otrar* (in Kazakh, Russian, and English). English translation by N. Golikov. Almaty: Rauan, 1997.

Olcott, Martha Brill. *The Kazakhs.* 2nd ed. [Palo Alto, California]: Hoover Institution Press, Stanford University, 1995.

Orazalinov, Sultan. *On the Land of Abai* (in Kazakh, Russian, and English). Almaty:Ōner, 1994.

*Otyrar sazy.* Produced in Astana by S. Baiterekov (artistic director) and T. Alpiev (producer). Compact disc.

Qasimanov, Sadyq. *Qazaq khalqynyng qoloneri* [Kazakh applied art (in Kazakh)]. Almaty: Qazaqstan, 1995.

Qongyratbaev, Auelbek, and Tynysbek Qongyratbaev. *Kone madeniet zhazbalary* [Written monuments of the ancient culture (in Kazakh)]. Almaty: Qazaq universiteti, 1991.

*Red Data Book of Kazakstan, The* (in Russian, with Kazakh and English summaries). Introduction by A. F. Kovshar. Compiled from material from the Republic of Kazakhstan's National Academy of Sciences, and the Ministry of Ecology and Bioresources; the Institute of

Zoology and Animal Gene Pools; and the Kazakhstan Central Asian Zoological Society. Almaty: Konzhyk, with funding from Chevron Overseas Company, 1996.

Reichl, Karl. *Turkic Oral Epic Poetry: Traditions, Forms, Poetic Structure.* New York: Garland Publishing, 1992.

Sakharieva, U. *The Traditional Weaving of Kazakhstan.* Almaty: Ōner, 1987.

Samashev, Zainolla. *Naskalnye izobrazheniia Verkhnego Priirtysh'ia* [Petroglyphs in the upper reaches of the Irtysh River (in Russian, with English summary)]. Alma-Ata: Ōner, 1992.

Sarybaev, Bolat. *Kazakhskie muzykalnye instrumenty* [Kazakh musical instruments: A study (in Russian)]. Alma-Ata: Zhalyn, 1978.

————. *Kazakhskie muzykalnye instrumenty* [Kazakh musical instruments: An illustrated album (in Russian)]. Alma-Ata: Zhalyn, 1978.

Seaman, Gary, ed. *Ecology and Empire: Nomads in the Cultural Evolution of the Old World.* Los Angeles: Ethnographics/USC, 1989.

Sicouri, Paola Pozzolini, and Vladimir Kopylov. *Forbidden Mountains: The Most Beautiful Mountains in Russia and Central Asia.* Italy: Indutech spa, 1994.

*Steppe Melodies: A Photo Album* (in Kazakh, Russian, and English). Edited by S. I. Novikova. Introduction by Mukhtar Shakhanov. Poetry by Abai Kunanbaev et al. Photographs by O. V. Belyalov et al. Alma-Ata: Kainar, 1987.

Svanberg, Ingvar, ed. *Contemporary Kazaks: Cultural and Social Perspectives.* Richmond, England: Curzon, 1999.

Sychova, Natalya. *Iuvelirnye ukrasheniia narodov Srednei Azii i Kazakhstana XIX–XX vekov: Iz sobraniia gosudarstvennogo muzeia iskusstva narodov Vostoka* [Traditional jewelry of the 19th and 20th centuries from Soviet Central Asia and Kazakhstan: From the collection of the museum of oriental art, Moscow (in English and Russian)]. Moscow: Sovetsky Khudozhnik, 1984.

Talanova, Olga, and Don Hinrichsen, comps. *The Aral, Yesterday and Now: Problems and Perspectives of Aral's Crisis* (in English and Russian). Translated by UNDP, Mariya Velzhanina, and Usagaly Dzhubangaliev. Edited by Svetlana Nikanova and Tatyana Nazarova. Photography by Oleg Belyalov, Yuri Kuidin, et al. Alma-Ata: МФСА, with support from the World Bank and the United Nations Development Programme (UNDP), 1997.

Tasmagambetov, Imanghali. *Jewellery Craft by Masters of Central Asia* (in Kazakh, Russian, and English). Almaty: Didar Publishing Company, 1997.

Tatimov, Makash. *Qazaq alemi* [The Kazakh world (in Kazakh)]. Almaty: Qazaqstan/ Atamyra, 1993.

————. *Xalyqnama: Nemese san men sana* [Demography: Numbers and consciousness (in Kazakh)]. Almaty: Zhazushy, 1992.

Thompson, Jon. *Oriental Carpets: From the Tents, Cottages and Workshops of Asia.* New York: E. P. Dutton, 1988; revised edition (London: Laurence King, 1993).

Tlemisov, Xaidulla Abdrahmanovich. *The National Cooking of the Kazakhs* (in Russian, German, and English). Alma-Ata: Kainar, 1990.

Tolybekov, Sultan. *Kochevoe obshchestvo Kazakhov v XVII–nachale XX veka* [Nomadic society of the Kazakhs from the 17th to the early 20th century (in Russian)]. Alma-Ata: Nauka, 1971.

Toqtabaeva, Shaizada. *Kazakh Jewelry* (in Kazakh, Russian, and English). Alma-Ata: Ōner, 1985.

Trofimova, Antonina. *Almaty and Environs.* Almaty: Rahat-Film, 1997.

Tursunov, Edyge. *Qazaq auyz adebietin zhasaushylardyng baiyrgy okilderi* [Ancient creator types in Kazakh oral literature (in Kazakh)]. Almaty: Ghylym, 1976.

————. *Vozniknovenie baksy, akynov, seri i zhyrau* [The origins of the baqsy, aqyn, seri and zhyrau (in Russian)]. Astana: Foliant, 1999.

Valikhanov, Chokan. *Sobranie sochinenij v 5–ti tomakh* [Collected works, 5 vols. (in Russian)]. Alma-Ata: Nauka, 1984–85.

Vostrov, Veniamin, and Marat Mukanov. *Rodoplemennoj sostav i rasselenie Kazakhov: Konets XIX–nachalo XX vekov* [The clan-tribe structure and settling of Kazakhs in the late 19th–early 20th centuries (in Russian)]. Alma-Ata: Nauka, 1968.

Vostrov, Veniamin, and Irina Zakharova. *Kazakhskoe narodnoe zhilishche* [Kazakh folk dwellings (in Russian)]. Alma-Ata: Nauka, 1989.

Vsevolodskaya-Golushkevich, Olga. *Baksy Oiyny* [Shaman's play (in Russian)]. Almaty: Rauan, 1996.

Winner, Thomas G. *The Oral Art and Literature of the Kazakhs of Russian Central Asia.* New York: Arno Press, 1980.

Yudin, Veniamin. "Ordy: Belaia, Siniaia, Seraia, Zolotaia…" [The Hordes: the White, the Blue, the Gray, and the Golden… (in Russian)]. In *Kazakhstan, Sredniaia I Tsentral'naia Aziia v XVI–XVIII vv.* [Kazakhstan and Central Asia in the 16th–18th centuries (in Russian)], edited by B. A. Tulepbaev, 106–65. Alma-Ata: Nauka, 1983.

Zakharova, Irina, and Rukiia Khodzhaeva. *Kazakhskaia natsional'naia odezhda: XIX–nachalo XX veka* [Kazakh national clothing: The 19th and early 20th centuries (in Russian)]. Alma-Ata: Nauka, 1964.

Zataevich, Aleksandr. *1000 pesen Kirgizskogo naroda: Napevy i melodii* [One thousand songs of the Kirghiz people: Tunes and melodies (in Russian)]. Orenburg: Kirgizskoe gosudarstvennoe izdatelstvo, 1925; reprinted in Russian as *1000 pesen Kazakhskogo naroda* [One thousand songs of the Kazakh people] (Moscow: Sovetskii kompozitor, 1963).

————. *500 Kazakhskikh pesen i kyuev Adaevskikh, Bukeevskikh, Semipalatinskikh i Uralskikh* [Five hundred songs and kyuis of Aday, Bukey, Semipalatinsk and the Ural Kazakhs (in Russian)]. Alma-Ata: Narkompros Kazakskoi ASSR, 1931; continuation of the author's *1000 pesen Kazakskogo naroda* [One thousand songs of the Kazakh people (in Russian)].

Zhanuzakova, Zaure, comp. *Kazakhskaia narodnaia instrumentalnaia muzyka: Kyui dlia dombry, kobyza i sybyzgi* [Kazakh instrumental folk music: Kyuis for dombra, kobyz and sybyzgy (in Russian)]. Alma-Ata: Ghylym, 1964.

Zharmukhamedov, M., ed. *XIX gasyrdagy Qazaq aqyndary* [Kazakh aqyns of the 19th century (in Kazakh)]. Almaty: Ghylym, 1988.

Zhubanov, Akhmet. *Kyui Kurmangazy* [The kyui of Kurmangazy (in Russian)]. Alma-Ata: Khudozhestvennaia literatura, 1961.

————. *Zamana bylbyldary* [Centuries of nightingales: Essays on the life and work of Kazakh folk composers/singers (in Kazakh)]. Almaty: Zhazushy, 1975; published first in Russian as *Solov'i stoletii: Ocherki o zhizni i tvorchetve Kazakhskikh narodnykh kompizitorov-pevtsov* (1967).

————. *Gasyrlar pernesi* [The strings of the centuries (in Kazakh)]. Almaty: Zhazushy, 1975; published first in Russian as *Struny stoletii* (Alma-Ata: Khudozhestvennaia literatura, 1956).

————. *An-Kyui sapary* [The journey of song and kyui (in Kazakh)]. Almaty: Ghylym, 1976.

————. *Kurmangazy Sagyrbaev: Omiri men tvorchestvosy* [Kurmangazy Sagyrbaev: Life and work (in Kazakh)]. Almaty: Zhalyn, 1978.

*This bibliography has been compiled from major sources used in preparation of the text and captions.

# ACKNOWLEDGMENTS

*The Soul of Kazakhstan* is the result of efforts over four years by a large number of people from a wide range of professions: alpinists, artists, writers, archeologists, anthropologists, culturalists, musicologists, historians, curators, librarians, researchers, shamans, Sufis, priests, equestrians, eagle hunters, drivers, helicopter pilots, and interpreters to name only a few.

The freedom, trust and financial support provided by ExxonMobil Kazakhstan, Inc. (EMKI), made the creation of this book possible. Gratitude to David Goodner, former vice president of Mobil Oil Kazakhstan, Inc. (MOKI), who envisioned and guided the project, and former president, Carl Burnett, is particularly due, as well as to current EMKI general manager, James Taylor, and Sharon Dey, formerly of Mobil Corporation. Special thanks must also be expressed to MOKI public relations coordinators Dana Suyundikova and Irina Serkebaeva for their invaluable and tireless help and contributions, and subsequently Dilyara Sydykova and Gulnara Iliusizova. Many of the MOKI staff supported the project in innumerable ways. Warm gratitude to Alexander Amelin, Saoule Amelina, Natalya Chemezova, Farit Kalimullin, Victor Khan, Sergei Korneev, Sergei Kryuchkov, Galina Lagunova, Arman Nurmukhanbetov, Oxana Satpaeva, Vitaly Vasilenko, and Natalia Vilensky.

The core team has worked with unrelenting dedication and commitment to make *The Soul of Kazakhstan* accurate, honest and respectful. Special thanks and acknowledgment to: Wayne Eastep, Alma Kunanbay, Gareth Steen, Patti Eastep, Bill McCaffery, William "D" DeVincenzo, Izaly Zemtsovsky, and our translators and consulting editors.

Language and graphics support in the Russian and Kazakh editions provided by Kasia Buczkowska, Stephan Gruben, Eric Jacobs, Greg Kapelyan, Mélanie Robinson, Gaukhar Sarsekeyeva, and Marat Tasmagambetov of Berlitz GlobalNET.

Advice, counsel and support from the following individuals help account for the breadth and depth brought to the book. Heartfelt appreciation to:

| | | | |
|---|---|---|---|
| Kayrat Abousseitov | Claudia Chang | Alexander Kolokolnikov | Nargiz Rakmanova |
| Alisher Akishev | Valentina Chebakova | Serikhan Kurmanov | Alexey Rogozhinsky |
| Kemal Akishev | Jane Coe | Galina Kush | Bakhytzhan Romankulov |
| Zukhra Akisheva | Kadisha Dairova | Baibosyn Kuzembaev | Suzanne Ross |
| Almas Alatau | Andrew Davis | Takhir Leonidovich | Zeinulla Samashev |
| Mukhamedzhan Aliev | Y. Dilmukhamedova | Vladimir Lukin | Jupar Sekbayeva |
| Zhannur Alimbayev | Boulat Djantaev | Nurbulat Masanov | Nurilya Shakhanova |
| Krym Altynbekov | Askar Esmakhanov | Alexander Mikhalevsky | Leila Sheriyazdanova |
| Yuri Aravin | Vladimir Filatov | Biket Momankulov | Vladimir Surtaev |
| Khalel Argynbayev | Ilíya Fishman | Kaltai Mukhamedjanov | Vladimir Suviga |
| Akmaral Arystanbekova | Faye Foster | Nurniyaz Mukhanov | Perry Tourtellotte |
| Andrei Astafyev | Burt Glinn | Galym Mutanov | Zholaoushy Turdugulov |
| Murat Auezov | Alexander Grishenko | Darkhan Mynbaev | Zhangir Umbetov |
| Aigul Azharova | Tolegen Ibraev | Moldakul Narumbetov | Baitursyn Umorbekov |
| Gulzada Bafina | Bek Ibrayev | Pavel Novikov | Cathy Wojtkun |
| Nikar Bafina | Amangul Ikhanova | Pernegul Omarova | Victor Zaibert |
| Karl Baipakov | Kuttykyz Ikhanova | Ainabek Ospanov | Dosbol Zhangalov |
| Temirkhan Baltabekov | Arkhimed Iskakov | Yuri Pachin | Yermek Zhangeldin |
| Aizhan Bekkulova | Dusen Kaseinov | Boris Preobrazhensky | Serik Zhanibekov |
| Natalya Beletskaya | Edward Kasinec | Timur Primbetov | Tamara Zhumaliyeva |
| Kabylbai Berdiyarov | Timur Kelmagambetov | Vladimir Proskurin | Vladimir Zolotaryov |
| Marshall Chamberlain | Almaz Khamzaev | Khadisha Rakimzhanova | |

THE COLORFUL **TUSKIIZ** USED AS THE BOOK'S FRONT ENDPAPER WAS EMBROIDERED BY ZAKIYA AKAI-KYZY. HER FAMILY MOVED TO MONGOLIA AFTER THE 1917 OCTOBER REVOLUTION AND THEY RETURNED TO KAZAKHSTAN IN 1998. HER EMBROIDERY INCORPORATES MONGOLIAN INFLUENCES IN HER KAZAKH STYLE. A **TUSKIIZ** IS A DECORATIVE WALL HANGING OR COVER.